RaT 28

Moving a House
with Preservation
in Mind

ABOUT THE SERIES

The American Association for State and Local History Book Series publishes technical and professional information for those who practice and support history and addresses issues critical to the field of state and local history. To submit a proposal or manuscript to the series, please request proposal guidelines from AASLH headquarters: AASLH Book Series, 1717 Church St., Nashville, Tennessee 37203. Telephone: (615) 320-3203. Fax: (615) 327-9013. Web site: www.aaslh.org.

ABOUT THE ORGANIZATION

The American Association for State and Local History (AASLH) is a nonprofit educational organization dedicated to advancing knowledge, understanding, and appreciation of local history in the United States and Canada. In addition to sponsorship of this book series, the Association publishes the periodical *History News*, a newsletter, technical leaflets and reports, and other materials; confers prizes and awards in recognition of outstanding achievement in the field; and supports a broad education program and other activities designed to help members work more effectively. To join the organization, contact: Membership Director, AASLH, 1717 Church St., Nashville, Tennessee 37203.

Moving a House with Preservation in Mind

PETER PARAVALOS

ALTAMIRA
PRESS

A Division of
ROWMAN & LITTLEFIELD PUBLISHERS, INC.
Lanham • New York • Toronto • Oxford

ALTAMIRA PRESS
A division of Rowman & Littlefield Publishers, Inc.
A wholly owned subsidiary of The Rowman & Littlefield Publishing Group, Inc.
4501 Forbes Boulevard, Suite 200
Lanham, MD 20706
www.altamirapress.com

PO Box 317
Oxford
OX2 9RU, UK

British Library Cataloguing in Publication Information Available

Library of Congress Cataloguing-in-Publication Data

Paravalos, Peter, 1967–
    Moving a house with preservation in mind / Peter Paravalos.
        p.   cm.— (American Association for State and Local History book series)
    Includes bibliographical references and index.
    ISBN-13: 978-0-7591-0956-8 (cloth : alk. paper)
    ISBN-10: 0-7591-0956-7 (cloth : alk. paper)
    ISBN-13: 978-0-7591-0957-5 (pbk. : alk. paper)
    ISBN-10: 0-7591-0957-5 (pbk. : alk. paper)
    1. Moving of buildings, bridges, etc.   2. Historic buildings—Conservation and
restoration.   3. Dwellings—Location.   I. Title.   II. Series.
    TH153.P283   2006
    690'.837—dc22   2005035906

Printed in the United States of America

♾ ™ The paper used in this publication meets the minimum requirements of
American National Standard for Information Sciences—Permanence of Paper for
Printed Library Materials, ANSI/NISO Z39.48–1992.

Contents

Acknowledgments

There are many individuals and organizations that I must thank for their assistance in producing this work. Through countless site visits, interviews, correspondences, and photographs, these individuals gave me the opportunity to learn and present much of the material in this book. Many structural movers are mentioned in the book but I would like to especially thank: Phil Marks of Atlantic AEolus, Bob Hayden of Hayden Building Movers, Don and Patricia Betts of D. R. Betts, Daniel Deitz of Deitz House Moving Engineers, Pat Burdette of Modern House & Building Movers, Mark and Stephen Edwards of Edwards Moving & Rigging, Jim Matyiko of Expert House Movers, Natalie Hammer of Ron Holland House Moving, Nickel Bros. House Moving, and International Chimney Corporation.

I would also like to thank the following individuals and organizations for their assistance and contributions: Tara Webber of Strawbery Banke, William Cashman of the Beaver Island Historical Society, Nicole Cloutier of the Portsmouth Public Library, John Atteberry of Boston College's John J. Burns Library, Joseph Cornish of Historic New England, Craig Tuminaro of the National Trust for Historic Preservation, Randy Wanger of PennDOT, David M. Knaebe of Hevi-Haul International, Marcia Starkey of Historic Greenfield, Joy Marks, Peter Beers, John E. Sharp, and Lois Anne (Zook) Mast.

Last, but certainly not least, I would like to thank my editor Susan Renaud. Susan's tireless queries, professional edits, and constant encouragement helped me put this work together in the manner presented. In closing, a loving thank you to my family: Mary Ellen, Sophia, and Peter.

Introduction

What is house moving, and what purpose does it serve? The thought of physically picking up a house, placing it on wheels, and rolling it down the street interests people to no end. If I were to describe the faces of onlookers witnessing a house being moved, I would have to say there is uncertainty, disbelief, and pure amazement. I have seen frustration as commuters wait in a convoy of moving equipment or for work crews to raise and lower utility lines. I have seen pedestrians, so stirred by what they are witnessing, that they stray into traffic without regard for their personal safety.

As a structural engineer, I understand what it takes to lift something of that size and magnitude. I had the fortunate experience of being involved with the relocation of the Highland Lighthouse in Truro, Massachusetts. The lighthouse and attached keepers dwelling were moved 450 feet away from the eroding bluffs, ultimately saving them from plummeting into the Atlantic Ocean. Working with the structural mover, I was able to gain further insight in the way structures of different shapes, sizes, and weights could be moved with relative ease. I later authored a technical paper titled "Moving an Historic Lighthouse," which I presented at a Technical Meeting for the Boston Society of Civil Engineers. The paper was later published in *Civil Engineering Practice*, the journal of the Boston Society of Civil Engineers Section/ASCE (American Society of Civil Engineers).

The Highland Lighthouse, located atop 140-foot bluffs in North Truro, Massachusetts, and lying within the Cape Cod National Seashore, is the oldest lighthouse on Cape Cod. The lighthouse, also known as Cape Cod Light, is listed on the National Register of Historic Places and was first situated in 1797 more than 500 feet from the edge of the imposing cliffs.

FIGURE I.1

The Highland Lighthouse being moved in 1995.

Photograph from Peter Paravalos and Wayne H. Kalayjian, "Moving an Historic Lighthouse," *Journal of the Boston Society of Civil Engineers Section/ASCE* 12, no. 2 (1997): 5–17.

During the 1790s, the federal government gradually assumed operation of existing lighthouses, completed several initially started by the states, and erected new ones. The administration of lighthouses became an accepted federal responsibility, located within the Treasury Department. In its early years, the establishment of lighthouses was directed by Congress as a result of private interest placing pressure on its members to introduce bills for lighthouse construction. It was in this manner that the Highland Light-house was established.

This lighthouse is the third lighthouse to be constructed at this location on the highlands of Truro. The first Cape Cod light was constructed out of timber with protective glass at the lantern deck. By the late 1840s, the Highland Lighthouse was nearing the end of its useful life and was rebuilt out of brick and stone. Four years later, the lighthouse was again rebuilt to accommodate visibility by southern approaching ships and had remained there for 140 years.

By the early 1990s, erosion, brought about by a string of severe winter storms, had claimed 400 feet of the shore line—forty feet in the last seven years prior to 1995. Alarmed by the progression of the eroding bluffs, the U.S. Coast Guard, which owned the lighthouse, together with local citizens and civic groups, actively campaigned to save the lighthouse from its destruction.

In 1994, a joint decision was made by the National Park Service and the Coast Guard to move the lighthouse further inland. The U.S. Congress therefore instructed the Coast Guard to oversee the relocation of the lighthouse. A year later, using a carefully planned and elaborate phased process, the Highland Lighthouse was moved 450 feet inland, saving it, at least for the foreseeable future, from severe coastal erosion.

Over the past thirty years, an increase in residential development in and around major cities, or urban sprawl, has created the need for buildable land and upgrades to infrastructure for commuting purposes.

In an effort to minimize commute time and maintain the standards of city life, neighborhoods in close proximity to major cities are prime candidates for development.

Since most of these neighborhoods are well established, there is a lack of developable land. Existing homes on expansive lots are purchased and demolished, and new larger homes with modern amenities are built in their place.

Events such as these have produced increases in house moves. Some 30,000 to 40,000 buildings are moved each year in the United States alone. The process, commonly referred to as "recycling," allows a house scheduled for demolition to be purchased and moved to another location. The house is reused, eliminating waste and saving much-needed landfill space.

A preservation campaign lead by the National Park Service has saved thousands of historically significant buildings throughout the United States (see chapter 4). Through the passing of the National Historic Preservation Act of 1966, the relocation of historic buildings has become quite common, particularly in the northeastern United States.

Other government efforts that have contributed to the increase in house moves are urban renewal and capital improvement. Urban renewal transforms impoverished urban neighborhoods through large-scale renovation or reconstruction, rehabilitating both housing and surrounding infrastructure (see chapter 9). Capital improvement programs consist of major upgrades to infrastructure through the widening of roadways, realignment of highways, and the addition of rail transit lines. To make way for these projects, homes are taken by eminent domain—government appropriation of private property for public use. Sometimes these houses are put on public auction or virtually given away at little or no cost to encourage relocating them.

Flooding and costal erosion are other reasons for moving a house. Nearly 7 percent of the U.S. land area is subjected to flooding. Relocating a house or raising it above flood levels may be the only option in avoiding flood damage. Coastal erosion resulting from beach–ocean interaction and intensified by storms has forced the moving of many homes and several lighthouses on the eastern seaboard.

The intent of this book is to examine the process of moving a house by discussing the planning stage, funding availability, moving options, the physical move, and cost analysis. A case study of Strawbery Banke in Portsmouth, New Hampshire, illustrates the importance of house moving in preserving the rich architectural heritage of this country. Finally, a chapter is devoted to providing examples of various house moves across the United States and the associated obstacles encountered by each. *Moving a House with Preservation in Mind* can be used as a reference to outline the many factors that must be considered when contemplating a house move and to assist in deciding whether to undertake such a complex project.

1

Moving Houses:
A History Lesson

Since the late 1800s, Americans have undertaken the complicated and delicate process of moving buildings. The concept has not changed; however, the means by which it is carried out certainly has. A house that rested on logs and was drawn by horses or oxen now rests on steel beams and is pulled by trucks or tractors. Historically, moving buildings was done for economic reasons. Today, circumstances have changed. A majority of building moves are carried out in an effort to save them from destruction. It is often easier and less expensive to raze an old building and construct a new one in its place than to move and rehabilitate the old one.

In a 1799 engraving by William Birch and Son (figure 1.1), a team of horses is shown moving a small timber-framed structure with the Walnut Street Jail in the background. The jail, situated directly opposite from the State House Yard, was designed by master builder/Architect Robert Smith in 1773–1774. Note the timber cross bracing used in preventing the racking or shifting of the structure and large wooden wheels presumably attached to a hefty wooden frame. This particular engraving is part of a set of twenty-eight others included in "The City of Philadelphia in the State of Pennsylvania, North America as it appeared in the Year 1800."

Figures 1.2, 1.3, and 1.4 depict an early version of a house move. Using screws or screw jacks, men would insert steel rods into a mechanism that would turn, raising a center shaft, thereby lifting the house (figure 1.2). Once high enough, wooden carriages three feet long, eighteen inches wide, and six inches square, with iron spikes and wheels, would be positioned under the sills of the house (figure 1.3). The screw jack would then be

1

FIGURE 1.1
Early move in Philadelphia in 1799.
Courtesy of the Library of Congress.

turned, lowering the house onto the carriages, which sat on wooden or iron rails. Finally, ropes wrapped around a steel pole capstan or rope-and-pulley system were tied to oxen or horses that pulled the house to the desired location (figure 1.4). As the structure moved forward, the rails would be picked up and reset ahead of the house.

As a civil engineer visiting the United States and Canada in the 1830s, David Stevenson was fascinated with the workings of house moving. He later published "Sketch of the Civil Engineering of North America," outlining in great detail his professional observations during his three-month tour.

Included in the book was a chapter devoted to house moving, specifically a four-story brick building located on 130 Chatham Street in New York City that measured twenty-five feet long by fifty feet wide. Stevenson commented on the high cost of American labor compared with British labor. He agreed with Americans that it made more economic sense to

FIGURE 1.2
House being raised by screws.
Illustration from *American Agriculturalist* 32 (November 1873). Courtesy of the John J. Burns Library, Boston College.

move a building that had required a significant investment in materials and labor to construct than to raze it and start over.

Using the two sketches depicted in figures 1.5 and 1.6, Stevenson described in detail the process of moving a four-story brick building back fourteen feet six inches to accommodate the widening of the street.

The Hotel Pelham was constructed in Boston in 1857, offering affordable accommodations conveniently located near the central business district. The hotel, modeled after a Parisian form of housing, was the first American apartment building and appeared to be a solution to the mid-nineteenth-century housing shortage in Boston.

Although the most popular architectural styles at the time were Italian-

FIGURE 1.3
Carriage for moving houses.
Illustration from *American Agriculturalist* 32 (November 1873). Courtesy of the John J. Burns Library, Boston College.

ate and Greek Revival, neither seemed appropriate for the location and scale of the building. Owner D. John H. Dix commissioned noted architect Alfred Stone to design the hotel to reflect the French Academic style. The mixed residential and commercial use building was located on the corner of Boylston and Tremont streets, facing Boston Common.

The 5,800-square-foot building was constructed out of freestone and brick. Freestone, usually made of sandstone or limestone, was produced without pronounced bedding planes and could, therefore, be worked equally well in any direction. The Hotel Pelham had two functioning entrances. The Tremont Street side of the building contained all the commercial entrances, while the more ornate Boylston Street side contained the entrances to the residents' apartments.

The first two floors of the Boylston Street facade consisted of paneled

FIGURE 1.4
A house being moved.
Illustration from *American Agriculturalist* (November 1873). Courtesy of the John J. Burns Library, Boston College.

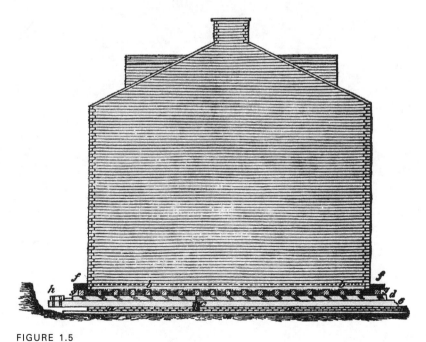

FIGURE 1.5
Preparing a foundation for a brick house in New York in the 1830s.
Illustration from David Stevenson, *Sketch of the Civil Engineering of North America* (London: J. Weale, 1838). Courtesy of the John J. Burns Library, Boston College.

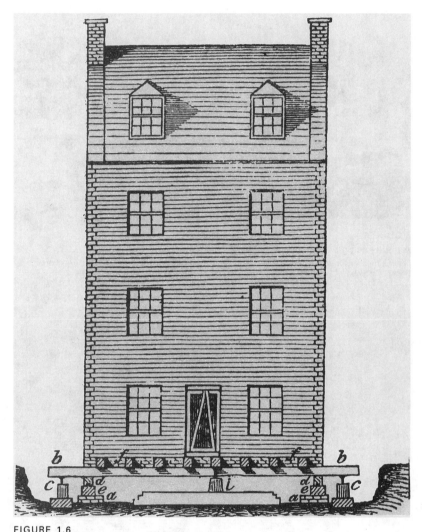

FIGURE 1.6
Preparing a foundation for a brick house in New York in the 1830s.

Illustration from David Stevenson, *Sketch of the Civil Engineering of North America* (London: J. Weale, 1838). Courtesy of the John J. Burns Library, Boston College.

FIGURE 1.7
Hotel Pelham, Boylston Street, Boston, Massachusetts, being moved in 1869.
Courtesy of Historic New England, formerly the Society for the Preservation of New England Antiquities.

pilasters that framed tall, arched store windows. The third through fifth floors contained apartments with tall, triple-sash windows enclosed by iron grilles. The sixth floor was surrounded by a low iron railing, and the top floor was enclosed within a mansard roof with recessed windows. Four large, rectangular oriel windows stood out on the Boylston Street facade.

The widening of Tremont Street in 1869 prompted the owner to move the hotel approximately fourteen feet west (figure 1.7). The project was considered the earliest instance of a large masonry building being moved.

The weight of the hotel was estimated at 5,000 tons, or 10 million pounds. It was moved using 904 rollers in combination with seventy-two screws pushing it along iron rails. The move, one inch every five minutes, took almost three months to complete. During that time, flexible tubing was used to maintain plumbing and gas service, so the first floor businesses and many of the apartment tenants remained in the residence.

In the years following the move, Boston residents took advantage of the increase in the number of streetcars enabling people to commute in and out of the city from their affordable homes in the suburbs and newly filled lands of the Back Bay. Residing in city apartment buildings became a last resort as a place to set up home.

The expansion of the Park Street trolley line, the demolition of the old Boston Public Library, and the dwindling commercial development in the area signaled the end for the Hotel Pelham. In 1916, it was demolished to make way for a new office building.

Newburyport, Massachusetts, is located on the south bank of the Merrimack River at the mouth of the Atlantic Ocean. Originally inhabited by Pawtucket Indians, Newbury was settled in the 1630s by European immigrants. The post quickly became a fishing and trading settlement, while the rest of Newbury turned to agriculture.

After breaking away from Newbury, Newburyport's economy prospered for a number of decades following the American Revolution. In 1811, a catastrophic fire destroyed the downtown, prompting the creation of a stringent fire code.

Today, the picturesque brick buildings and cobblestone roads remind visitors of the proud history of this thriving New England port.

Figure 1.8 illustrates the use of oxen to pull a house down State Street through the center of town. The man on the roof of the building grabs overhead wires lifting them over the peak.

FIGURE 1.8
House being moved down State Street, Newburyport, Massachusetts.
Photograph by George Noyes. Courtesy of Historic New England, formerly the Society for the
Preservation of New England Antiquities.

In perhaps the most remarkable move to date, the Captain Samuel
Brown Mansion in Brown's Station, Pennsylvania, was moved vertically
up a 160-foot sheer hillside (figure 1.9). The house was originally built on
the edge of the Monongahela River in 1868 by Captain William Brown,
Samuel's father.

In 1903, the mansion needed to be relocated to accommodate the
realignment of the Baltimore & Ohio Railway. James Ward Jr., a descendant of the Brown family, sold the land to B&O and, in an emotional
decision, requested the house to be moved up the cliff face to an elevation
160 feet above its former site.

The house weighed roughly 180 tons and measured eighty-five feet by
forty feet. The initial task was to shore up the house and prepare it for
lifting. This was achieved by inserting 200 seven-inch steel needle beams
beneath the structure, followed by eight large timbers, measuring twelve
by sixteen inches and eighty-five feet in length, beneath the needle beams.

At the same time, the cliff was excavated in four locations along its

FIGURE 1.9
Captain Samuel Brown's Mansion, Brown's Station, Pennsylvania.
Courtesy of the Carnegie Library of Pittsburgh.

height, creating four shelves thirty feet in height. Next, the house was raised by hand jacks located on stacked cribbing that formed eight walls beneath the eight large timbers that supported the needle beams. Each timber in the stacks of cribbing measured six by eight inches. To prevent the racking or shifting of the cribbing walls from side to side, eight- by eight-inch timber members were threaded between the stacks perpendicularly and fastened with chains and turnbuckles.

When the house had been lifted thirty feet, it was pulled onto the first shelf by means of two winches using two-inch lines containing four-part blocks mounted at the top of the cliff. Each winch was powered by two horses. Another lift of thirty feet was made to the next shelf, and the process was repeated until the house was set on its new site, 200 feet back from and 160 feet above the old site.

The move cost $40,000, exceeding the original cost to construct the house. It required an estimated 20,000 carefully sized timbers and beams that were transported to the site in twenty railroad cars. Unfortunately, after such a remarkable achievement in engineering and preservation, the house was totally destroyed by fire in 1913.

In 1920, it was discovered that nearly one-third of the town of Hibbing, Minnesota, was sitting atop an estimated 25 million tons of iron ore. This prompted one of the most extensive relocation efforts in the United States. The Oliver Iron Mining Company moved a majority of the structures located in a sixteen-block area to other parts of the town and to neighboring Alice, Minnesota. The project, which took about three years to complete, required not only a great deal of manual labor but also the skill and expertise of moving structures. The Colonial Hotel shown in figure 1.10 was one of the largest structures moved. The Sellers Hotel, a similar three-story framed building, was not so lucky. According to a local paper, "the building started to slip away from the road; it slid over to one side and then fell to pieces."

The picture also demonstrates the magnitude of the buildings that were moved and the types of equipment used to carry out such an undertaking. Steam locomotive tractors with traction belts, heavy logs, jacks, and horse-drawn wagons were commonly used at the time. As in most building moves, photographs capture the overwhelming feeling of accomplishing the impossible.

FIGURE 1.10
The Colonial Hotel being moved in Hibbing, Minnesota, in 1920.
Courtesy of the Minnesota Historical Society.

Located some twenty miles from the mainland in Lake Michigan, Beaver Island has a year-round population of 450 people and is rich in history and tradition. It is believed that the island's original inhabitants were the Odawa (Ottawa) Native Americans. Because of the island's abundant forests and ample fishing, it became a home to traders and trappers in the early 1800s.

The island's economy flourished in part from the ongoing logging industry but mostly from fishing; by the mid-1880s, Beaver Island had become the largest supplier of freshwater fish in the country. Eventually, overfishing and the arrival of the lamprey eel caused the demise of the fishing industry in the 1940s.

In the late 1970s, with the economy of Michigan improving, tourism sparked an interest in Beaver Island, and people bought property and built homes in record numbers. Seeing an increase in lake travel, the U.S. government was charged with erecting a series of lifesaving stations around the Great Lakes. Some twenty-eight stations would be required, but with

FIGURE 1.11
Beaver Island, Whiskey Point, Life-Saving Quarters, 1970.
Courtesy of the Beaver Island Historical Society.

a lack of comparable buildings for such a task, the government was forced
to purchase train station buildings from a company in Chicago. The company added a widow's walk to offer a more elegant model, but this was
not well received.

The Whiskey Point Life-Saving Quarters was originally located near the
lighthouse manned by Elizabeth Whitney Williams, Michigan's first
female lighthouse keeper. The building was decommissioned in the 1950s,
and there it stood for twenty years before Charlie Martin, a third-genera-
tion Beaver Island fisherman who had stuck it out through the island's
downturn, bought the building and announced that he would "skid it"
(apply grease to timber planking and push or pull the building over the
greased timbers) to his property a mile away on the harbor at St. James.
Able to be moved only a few hundred feet, the station was left in the road
until a county plow truck was able to push it the rest of the way to his
property.

Charlie passed away a year after the above photo was taken, and his son Ernie took over the fishing business in the late 1970s. He then sold the Quarters and had it moved half a mile away, where it is currently being used as a residence with most of the Quarter's architectural features preserved for generations to come.

2

Decision Making

The decision whether to move a house can be daunting, and the home owner must ask him- or herself many questions. What is the purpose of the move? Is the move preservation related? Is the structure's history, construction, or architecture significant? Will the house be renovated, rehabilitated, or restored? Can I find an acceptable new site? Will the benefits outweigh the cost (and stress) of moving my house? Answers to questions such as these will determine what part moving the house will play in the overall project.

Once it is decided that the house will be moved, it is important to develop an understanding of the moving process, to determine the extent of the role that the structural mover will play, and to have a clear grasp of your responsibilities as a home owner.

One of the most important aspects of a successful project is the selection of a qualified, experienced structural mover. The sooner in the process they become involved, the better your chances of bringing the project in on time and on budget.

This book will aid in educating and guiding individuals who are interested in moving a house and help devise a relocation plan.

THE CASE AGAINST MOVING

What is happening now in Vermont and New Hampshire clearly illustrates one case against moving a building. Currently, barns are bought by the wealthy, professionally dismantled, shipped to other parts of the country, reassembled, and used for their historic significance and eclectic value. What are left behind are huge voids or cutouts in the surrounding landscape and historic fabric where the barns once stood.

Unlike covered bridges and stone walls, barns are not protected by laws preventing their destruction or removal. In the case of Vermont and New Hampshire barns, they are not in danger of being destroyed but rather are in need of continued upkeep to ensure their survival. Proposed legislation in both states will require owners of barns more than seventy-five years old to offer towns and cities the right of first refusal before a sale to another party can take place.

THE CASE FOR MOVING

There are many benefits in moving a house: economic, environmental, preservation, and even sentimental. Economically, it is usually cheaper to move an existing house than it is to build a new one. Construction costs in 2004 averaged about $135 per square foot or more, and renovation costs are even higher. In some instances, the cost of moving and resettling into a house can be 30 to 50 percent less than the cost of a new house.

As a state and local tax advantage, rather than demolishing the house and losing valuable taxes, the structure could be recycled and sold at a below-market value and relocated, maintaining the tax base. Developer's can save $5,000 to $10,000 in demolition and disposal costs and still profit from developing the vacated site.

As an example, when a house is demolished, the taxes that are paid on that property are reduced since the site no longer contains a dwelling. Until a new house is constructed, months or even years of taxes could be lost. However, if the original house on that property is relocated, the taxes on the new piece of land where the house is set would increase, thus reestablishing the tax base.

Environmentally speaking, the average structure produces about 100 cubic yards of building material waste; recycling a house means less waste dumped into our dwindling landfill space. With a single tree producing approximately 100 board feet of lumber and the average structure requiring roughly 5,000 board feet of lumber, the savings translate to fifty trees saved per structure moved. Multiply this by an estimated 35,000 buildings in the United States moved per year, and the number of trees saved is 1.75 million.

Historic preservation, saving a house from demolition for its historic significance, has increased over the years largely because of the availability of government-sponsored grants and tax benefits. Historical societies, civil groups, and concerned citizens often undertake such projects to safeguard the history of their cities and towns.

Perhaps your family's needs have outgrown the house you love so much, but your lot cannot accommodate an addition. Maybe the solid and stately home built by your great-great-grandfather is located on a heavily traveled roadway. Instead of selling the entire property and moving to a new home, you can bring your house and memories to a site that allows for expansion or has a more desirable location.

In short, owners who donate structures destined for demolition to an interested party help encourage preservation, save much-needed landfill space, and possibly obtain a tax credit.

MOVING A HOUSE

When deciding if moving a house is a viable option, many factors need to be considered. For starters, there are several questions that must be answered that will help you come to a decision regarding a potential move:

1. What is the condition and makeup of the house?
2. What is the historical nature of the house, if any?
3. What is the route over which the move will traverse?
4. Where is the site, and what is its topography?
5. What will the move cost?

After considering these questions, with the help of your structural mover and the local historical commission (if appropriate), an informed decision can be made on the project's feasibility, and the planning for the move can begin.

Condition and Makeup of a House

For starters, the more deteriorated the house is, the more expensive and limited your moving options may be. Houses that are set to be demolished and are put up for public auction typically require major rehabilitation. In fact, if the house is in poor condition, a move may be out of the question. This is one reason that a structural mover should be consulted as early in the process as possible.

The construction of your house and type of building materials used will also dictate the type and cost of the move. A timber-frame house will likely be easier and less expensive to move than a brick veneer house, primarily because of its lighter weight. A timber-frame house can be cut up into smaller sections, while a brick house must be moved in one piece. This presents a much greater challenge, as the larger size and weight will need to be accommodated by the structural mover, more specialized equipment will be required, and more costs will pass down to the home owner.

Historical Significance of a House

If the house you plan on moving has no historical relevance and will not be relocating in a historic district, then your task may be a bit easier. However, if the house is historic and is located in or is moving to a historic district, the steps you will take in your moving process will be different. Not only is government funding available for such moves, but there are also rules and regulations one must follow. This will be covered in detail in chapters 3 and 4.

The original tavern "The Sign of the Kings Arms" was occupied by James Stoodley, a sea captain at one time, but burned down several years

FIGURE 2.1
Stoodley's Tavern, Strawbery Banke, Portsmouth, New Hampshire.
Courtesy of the author.

after it opened. It was frequented at the time by the famous Major Robert Rogers of the British Rangers who often recruited men to fill the ranks of the British Crown. In 1761, the new "Stoodley's Tavern" was built on the site of a former tavern of the same design and shape. It was at this tavern that men gathered to plan and carry out treasonable raids on Fort William and Mary on Great Island against the British in 1774.

Legend also has it that it was at Stoodley's that women of Portsmouth met to stitch together the first American flag, which flew from the masthead of John Paul Jones's warship. That same flag was the first flag to be saluted by a foreign warship.

The building was scheduled to be torn down to make way for a new federal building and post office in downtown Portsmouth. A nonprofit organization raised more than $20,000 in 1966 and had the building moved from 125 Daniel Street to the Strawbery Banke parcel (see chapter 8).

The Transport Route

This is perhaps the most important part of a move. The route you choose to take in moving your house can make or break a project. A move over water is dramatically different than one over land. The cost of moving over water is considerably higher, but this may be the only option if the project is to proceed (see chapter 7).

There are many obstacles one must overcome when moving over land. The same holds true in moving over water. You can just imagine watching your house rolling down the street, under the bridge, through town, across a six-foot-wide road, and uphill to your new house lot.

Power lines, trees, fences, buildings, bridges, overpasses, and traffic lights are just some of the hurdles that structural movers face when planning the transport route over land. Over water, there are tidal, wind, aquatic plant, and even migratory bird concerns, just to name a few.

If you plan on moving on your existing house lot to distance your home from a busy street, for instance, the moving process should be much easier.

The New Site

The new site refers to the location where the house will finally be situated. Site preparation will typically include land clearing to facilitate moving the house into position and pouring the new foundation.

FIGURE 2.2
A house being moved along the beach.
Courtesy of Hayden Building Movers, Cotuit, Massachusetts.

In most cases, the new foundation, which will support the house, will need to be built after the house is situated over its final resting place. Also keep in mind that once the house is moved to the new site, water, electrical, and waste disposal systems will need to be installed. All of this can take weeks or even months if not carefully scheduled.

Most of the time, the physical move itself takes less time than the logistics of putting the house back together. If the house needs a great deal of work to be reconstructed, this will take considerable time and money.

Associated Costs

There are a variety of costs associated with a house move. There is the cost of the new land where the house will be placed, permitting costs, moving costs, alternative living arrangement costs, dumping costs associated with the old foundation, and costs to ready the new site. Don't forget the time and effort required in planning and executing the move. A breakdown and estimate of total costs can be found in chapter 8.

The Moving Process: What's Involved

There are several steps that have to be taken before the actual move of the house. The first and most important is obtaining permission to move the structure. This is the initial stage in getting a house moved and is often called the permitting stage. Getting all the required permits will avert legal opposition and avoid unnecessary obstacles in your project. The permitting stage often takes longer than the move itself.

Permitting in essence notifies all affected parties of the project and helps address unforeseen difficulties that, if discovered late in the project, could stall the move indefinitely and increase costs. For example, many cities and towns have set times when a house can be moved. On Cape Cod, Massachusetts, road projects, including a house move, are not allowed on public streets during the summer season, specifically between mid-June and mid-September. The reasons are clear. The population on the island of Nantucket, off the coast of Cape Cod, is roughly 7,000 people in the winter but balloons to 40,000 in the summer.

The influx of vacationers makes it very difficult for vehicular traffic to navigate the island's crowded streets. A house move at any hour of the day would be asking for gridlock.

The permitting stage is usually handled by your structural mover. It is essential that the mover be chosen as early as possible so that while waiting for permissions they can study the structure and develop the relocation plan.

SELECTING A STRUCTURAL MOVER

Selecting the right structural mover for the job is certainly the most important decision one will make in this entire process. There are three requirements that will dictate your choice of moving contractor: time line, type of move, and type of house. Your time line refers to a required deadline by which the house must be moved. This can be based on a scheduled demolition, funding requirements, real estate transactions, or just a personal decision.

Type of move can mean a number of things: historic house move, overland or over-water move, dismantled or partial move, lot or distance move, and complicated or easy move. Chapter 5 discusses each type of move in detail.

House type refers to the size and shape of the house and the material used in constructing it. Moving a stick or conventional lumber house is considerably different than moving a masonry or brick house.

It is in your best interest to select a structural mover whose experience reflects both your house type and the type of move. The process of selecting a moving contractor can be broken down into two parts: investigation and contract.

Investigation Phase

The best place to start your search is with the International Association of Structural Movers (IASM) at www.iasm.org. This site breaks down movers by state to help you find a mover near you. It is important to find a local mover specifically in terms of the required permitting and utility work associated with your project. Local movers are familiar with town officials and townspeople, and this sometimes proves to be more important than the move itself. Such movers deal with town officials, municipalities, and utilities on a regular basis. Having a connection at the town hall, police department, or department of public works can save the project a considerable amount of time and even money.

Many movers often have their own websites depicting past moves and providing contact information. The IASM website lists movers in the United States and Canada. In chapter 9, six movers are showcased in a variety of projects. After you have selected at least three prospective movers, the following is a list of questions that will help narrow your search:

1. Does the contractor hold a valid license to move structures, in good standing with the department of transportation? In some states, a license is required only if you are traveling over state highways. How-

ever, it should be noted that if your contractor is unlicensed and an accident occurs on the job, you may be held liable for deaths, injuries, or property damage.

2. Does the contractor carry liability insurance? If so, what does it cover, what is excluded, and what is the limit of the liability? Liability insurance covers injury to people or property, including the house while in the care of the moving contractor. At a minimum, the mover should carry workers' compensation and liability insurance of $2,000,000.

3. Is the contractor's insurance premium paid to date? If lapses in a mover's coverage occur, they are required by law to notify the state department of transportation. Recouping damages from an unlicensed, uninsured mover can be costly, time consuming, or even impossible.

4. Should you purchase riders to your home-owner's insurance to cover unforeseen damage, such as cracks in walls, water damage, theft, or vandalism? Additional riders cover exclusions in the mover's liability insurance (follow up with your insurance agent).

5. What kind of moves does the contractor accept? Some structural movers may perform only lot moves. This avoids the permitting process of a distance move and allows the contractor to fill his schedule with more moves that are less time consuming.

6. Is the contractor experienced with your type of move? It's always best to hire a firm with relevant experience, especially in a historic house move. Request photographs of previous projects to verify that the company has moved historic structures.

7. Has the local building department worked with this company? Was the mover's work capable or questionable? If you find that a department may have rejected a move, find out why. Check the building departments of other towns where the mover has worked.

8. Will the mover provide references? A reputable company should be glad to. References should give a good indication of the company's professionalism and quality of prior work. Select references whose project was most similar to yours. Don't be afraid to ask tough questions such as "Would you hire this company again?" Most people are willing to help. If a previous client is unwilling to answer any questions, it could be a "red flag," and more investigation should be done.

9. Are there complaints against the company? Check with the Better

Business Bureau, the mover's union, or the IASM to see if there have been any complaints lodged or penalties issued against the mover. If there are and you are still interested, you might want to check on why and the severity of the complaints.

10. What does the estimate cover? Is there a fee for the estimate? You should expect to pay for a consultation to determine if your move is feasible even if you do not select that contractor. Often the estimate is deducted from the cost of the move.

11. For how long is the quote good? A quote is usually valid for ninety days.

12. Does the moving contractor require a percentage of payment in advance? Typically, you will be required to pay a nonrefundable deposit to reserve a spot on the mover's schedule, a portion due on the day work commences, payment prior to setting the house on its new foundation, and a final installment when the work is complete.

Contract Phase

Because of the complexity of moving a structure, you should not select a company solely because it is the lowest bidder. Often, you get what you pay for. Your decision should be based on quality of work and relevant experience, with price as a third factor. Try to strike a balance among all three, giving price the least amount of weight.

The contract that is drafted must outline contractor and owner responsibilities. It should include most situations that may arise while your house is in the care of the moving contractor. Issues such as weather delays, damages, vandalism, and even rental fees must be addressed prior to signing a contract.

Rental fees may be incurred if delays in your move should occur. For example, a delay in pouring the new foundation may interfere with the mover's ability to proceed to his next scheduled move. The equipment needed for the next job is supporting your house while the new foundation is being poured. This creates a problem for the mover. The mover may charge you a rental fee for his equipment or even charge you for renting additional equipment. To avoid situations like this, read the contract carefully and offer suggestions to clarify responsibility in unforeseen events.

PERMITTING

Prior to any house move, whether it traverses a public road, is over water, or is a lot move, proper permits must be obtained. This process can take from one to three months, depending on your situation. If the house is very large or the move is long, permitting may take more than a year. If the move is an emergency or is required because of eminent domain or erosion, the process can be sped up. The route of the move and by what means it will be carried out will define your permitting requirements.

Most cities and towns across the United States have permitting requirements. The best place to obtain a list of requirements is your local building department, construction services department, or building inspector. Permits must be obtained from every community the house travels through.

Following is a typical list of structure relocation authorization requirements; although these may vary from state to state, the majority will apply:

1. *Application and plans.* A licensed general contractor is required to submit plans and an application for a permit to move and relocate the structure. A fee is paid, and proof of insurance meeting the town's requirements must be presented by the contractor. Every town is different, and the amount of insurance coverage will vary. Usually the building code officer, chief of police, and director of the department of public works (DPW) review the application and two sets of plans. Each set must contain the following: new site plan, zoning, setbacks, foundation, connections to new foundation, and the location of tie-ins for plumbing and electrical service.

2. *Historical commission approval.* If the building is in a historic district, being relocated into one, or listed on the National Register, a letter of approval must be obtained from the historic preservation planner; in addition, procedures should be followed as outlined in chapter 5.

3. *Professional structural engineer certification letter.* This is a signed and sealed letter from a registered structural engineer describing the structural integrity of the house to be moved.

4. *Soils engineer certification letter.* This is a letter from a geotechnical engineer certifying that the soil at both the old site and the new site is capable of supporting the structure to be moved.

5. *Approval from the zoning board of appeals.* The zoning board of appeals conducts hearings for property owners or prospective buyers request-

ing a variance or deviation from zoning ordinances or an interpretation of the ordinance language. Applicants for a variance submit an application and supporting documentation. A notice of public hearing is sent to all property owners within 300 feet of the property in consideration. The zoning board of appeals' members conduct a public hearing and make a decision to approve or deny the request.

6. *Building permit obtained from the building department.* A building permit is required when one erects, constructs, enlarges, alters, moves, repairs, improves, converts, or demolishes any building or structure. The processing of the permit application will vary with the seasonal workload and complexity of your project.

7. *Performance bond.* You must determine whether a bond is required for any phase of the project. A bond (or performance bond, as they are sometimes called) is an amount of money that you provide to the town prior to obtaining the permit. The town can then use the bond money for costs incurred by the city as a result of the move, such as police and department of public works personnel, damages to public property, signage replacements, or cleanup. After costs are assessed, the remainder of the bond is refunded.

8. *Electrical and plumbing letter.* This is a letter from licensed electrical and plumbing contractors to secure permits for all work and to approve the condition of the wiring and plumbing system.

9. *Permits and releases from the following:*

   a. *Department of transportation.* The mover must provide the department of transportation (DOT) with a description of the structure to be moved, the size, the maximum height when loaded and ready to be moved, the maximum width of the structure in the direction of travel, and the kind of equipment to be used by the mover to carry out the move. The DOT can then determine areas along the route where street structures may need to be removed, including sidewalks, curbing, fire hydrants, street signs, and signals and whether any trees will require trimming. The DOT will then make a determination on which bridges and streets the structure can and cannot traverse over or under depending on the axle load and right-of-way limitations.

      The DOT will also decide the days of the week a move can take place and the time of day. Typically, a move will be authorized

between 2:00 A.M. and 5:00 A.M. on weekdays only, excluding holi-
days. A minimum of six weeks is required to obtain the permit.

In this picture, the structural mover is required to take a serpen-
tine path to get onto Mt. Vernon Street in the foreground. This
required several utilities to raise, lower, connect, and disconnect
wires; traffic control; and precision maneuvering by the driver of
the truck. This picture shows the first truck in a series of five. This
first truck had the tallest and widest load used to calculate clearances
and therefore was placed at the head of the line. All the subsequent
trucks carried smaller portions of the house. This area alone took
forty-five minutes for the convoy of moving vehicles to pass
through.

b. *Railroad crossings.* Depending on the dimensions of the house, railroad signage, signals, and wires may need to be removed. The company controlling the tracks will specify a time frame during which
the house can be moved across the tracks. This is done so as not to
affect train schedules, often between 8:00 P.M. and 6:00 A.M. In some
cases, the railroad company may accommodate other times.

FIGURE 3.1
A house moving through the streets of Nantucket, Massachusetts.
Courtesy of the author.

c. *Police and fire departments.* The police department will determine if the route of the move adversely affects traffic or compromises public safety. The department will also provide police details and No Parking signs to control traffic flow in public streets and to clear the path for the moving trucks. In addition, if the move will require the temporary removal of wires attached to fire alarm or police signal systems, permits and estimates for temporary removal of these wires must be obtained.

d. *Department of public works, cable, telephone, and electric companies.* These four entities make up the utilities associated with a move over public streets. The mover should be mindful that each utility is responsible for its own wires. This means as many as eight different utility trucks, two from each utility, assisting in temporary wire displacement and removal. One truck takes down the overhead lines, while the other puts them back in place after the house has cleared the wires. Miscommunication and poor planning can prolong the move and translate into additional costs to the mover, which in turn are passed on to the owner. There should be constant activity throughout the move. If you notice the moving crew standing and waiting, be prepared for a delay in the schedule, possibly extending the move into another day, with an increase in costs.

Utility companies can handle only their respective lines. This can slow a move considerably. The key to any move that requires a considerable amount of utility work is the scheduling of multiple teams to raise, lower, detach, and reattach wires. While one team disconnects, the other should be disconnecting farther up the line. As the convoy passes each utility point, the wires may be reconnected by a subsequent team, thus keeping the mover's vehicles constantly rolling.

e. *Environmental Protection Agency.* The role of the Environmental Protection Agency (EPA) is to ensure that the natural environment is not adversely affected in any way. The name may vary from state to state; in Florida, the Department of Environmental Protection performs the same function. If the route of the move crosses or comes dangerously close to wetlands or endangered plant or animal species, permits from the EPA are required.

FIGURE 3.2
Cable, telephone, and electric utilities.
Courtesy of the author.

Typically, moving permits are the responsibility of the mover, while building permits are that of the owner. If the move requires the use of public streets, the mover will obtain an "over-the-road permit" and charge you for the permit as well as his time and effort in getting it. A way to save money may be to secure the permit yourself and save several hundred dollars. This may sound tempting, but don't forget that the mover is experienced in obtaining these permits and that what may seem simple at first could turn out to be a logistical nightmare. Although there are money-saving shortcuts in the moving process, this one is not recommended.

In addition to permitting, an advertisement must be written in the local paper notifying the town of the day and time of the move and the route that the house will take. This is done at least one month in advance, with an additional reminder published a couple of days before the move.

HOME-OWNER REQUIREMENTS AND RESPONSIBILITIES
One of the first tasks of the structural mover will be to perform a condition survey of the house by inspecting framing members, sills, and utili-

ties. In most cases, the mover will provide a list of required upgrades and suggested improvements to the home owner. All upgrades must be completed prior to any work performed by the mover. The mover can often perform all required work, but, of course, these costs plus disposal fees will be incurred by the home owner.

Some typical requirements include the following:

1. *Replacement of sills and framing members.* Any sills or framing members that may be rotted and could jeopardize the move will need to be replaced prior to the arrival of the structural mover. In most cases, the mover can provide a list of contractors he has worked with in the past that can perform the work.

2. *Utility disconnection.* Utilities such as water, sewer, gas, electric, telephone, and cable must be disconnected. The water, sewer, and gas services must be properly capped at the service shutoff, and wires, including electric, telephone and cable, must be removed. In Massachusetts, Maine, New Hampshire, Rhode Island, and Vermont, a structural mover will not enter the site unless Dig Safe® has been on-site and has marked any underground utility lines.

   Dig Safe System, Inc., is a not-for-profit corporation funded entirely by member utility companies to promote public safety and safeguard against property and environmental damage. With one phone call, the home owner informs Dig Safe® of a proposed excavation site. Dig Safe® then notifies member companies of the proposed excavation project. The member utilities survey the work area and identify the location of underground facilities at no expense to the home owner. This call should be made at least two months in advance.

3. *Furnace and oil tank removal.* Unless stated in the contract, the furnace and oil tank are not removed by the structural mover. It is the responsibility of the home owner to hire someone to remove this equipment. One way to save money may be for the home owner to perform this task. Any basement appliances that the home owner wishes to keep, such as a washer and dryer, must also be removed.

4. *Plumbing.* A determination must be made by the home owner on what plumbing is to be saved or discarded. Anything that extends past the bottom of the framing members must usually be removed.

5. *Tree and shrub removal.* The home owner may save money by removing

shrubs and small trees that are planned for replanting at the new site. If the mover does it, the home owner will be responsible for any associated costs.

The home owner should be aware that it is common for the mover to require a six-foot clearance around the perimeter of the house. Earthen ramps may be required to accommodate earthmoving equipment that will break up the existing foundation and accommodate lifting beams to be placed below the house. This perimeter may have trees, shrubs, or other items in the way. It is the home owner's responsibility to instruct the mover what is to be moved and what will be discarded. Either way, the owner incurs the cost. The cost of moving a mature tree can be as much as $600. If the tree is to be moved away from the house and then returned to its former location, the cost is doubled.

Some typical responsibilities include the following:

1. *Home-owner condition survey.* The home owner should survey the house and photograph and record existing wall cracks and damage prior to the move (see chapter 5).
2. *Personal possession packing.* It is recommended but not required that the home owner pack up all breakables, such as glassware, china, and wall hangings, as well as valuable items. If an unforeseen incident occurs and the move is postponed, valuables could be left unattended and may fall victim to burglary or vandalism.
3. *Alternative living arrangements.* The actual move may only take one day, but the entire moving process can take months. It is recommended that alternative living arrangements be made.

   Sometimes living arrangements planned for three weeks turn into three months. The house in figure 3.3 sat in Chatham Harbor waiting for arrangements to be made for the completion of its journey.

ROUTE PLANNING

Your travel route will be determined by how the house will be moved (in one piece or several pieces) and how successful the mover is in the permitting stage. It is not uncommon for a move to be turned down, canceled, or otherwise stalled in the permitting stage. Some reasons for this may include the following:

FIGURE 3.3
A house in Chatham Harbor, Cape Cod, Massachusetts.
Courtesy of Hayden Building Movers, Cotuit, Massachusetts.

1. *Utilities.* If the house move requires the temporary removal of utilities, the cost to do this may outweigh the cost of the move itself. This is the case in all states except Massachusetts. Based on a court decision in 1979, the air rights, or right-of-way in the airspace twenty feet from the centerline of the roadway on either side and straight up into the sky, is owned by the state; therefore, if utility lines obstruct transportation, the utilities are responsible for removing and resetting their lines at their own expense.

   For many years, the IASM has been challenging the utility companies seeking to enact the Massachusetts court decision nationwide but so far has been unsuccessful.

   Tree trimming for utility adjustments can slow the moving process and stretch a day's work into possibly two or three. It is imperative that the mover check with utilities prior to moving day to determine whether a drive through and clearing of the proposed route has taken place.

2. *Neighboring communities.* Some town or city boards may turn down projects that may be considered too disruptive or otherwise undesir-

able. For example, moving a house through the town business center disrupts power and other utilities, potentially causing a financial hardship to local businesses.

3. *Obstructions.* A high-quality structural mover will drive the entire move route, taking notes and measurements of all the possible obstructions. Usually, trees and shrubs along the travel route are trimmed to minimize damage to the siding of the house. In some cases, there may be something in the way of the move that cannot be temporarily relocated or otherwise removed. When dealing with historic districts, the houses are not the only things worth saving. Trees can be as old if not older than the house being moved and can create a barrier that cannot be crossed.

4. *Infrastructure.* If the house is moved on public roadways, the bridges and roadways associated with supporting the moving vehicles may alter your route or mode of transportation. The collective weight of the house, the steel beams supporting it, and the vehicle hauling it may exceed the posted weight limit of a bridge. An alternative route may need to be used.

   Often, houses are wider than the bridges they are traversing. This may cause a portion of the house to come dangerously close to the top of the bridge railing system. The height at which the house sits in relation to the surface of the road is very important and is why accurate route planning and measurements are imperative.

   If public streets pose a problem with the move, a barge may be an alternative if the house is situated adjacent to a river, lake, or ocean. With a barge, utilities and obstructions may be avoided, but some public permits may still be required. Unless you are located right on the water, off-loading a house onto public property will require permits. Additional permitting will consist of water transport and environmental permitting. Bridge clearances, currents, tides, and weather must also be considered and planned for accordingly (see chapter 7).

THE NEW SITE

Prior to the arrival of the house to the new site, there are a number of tasks that must be completed. The following list can be used as a guide:

1. *Building permit.* Work cannot commence at the new site without a building permit. This permit is obtained at the initial or subsequent

FIGURE 3.4
A tight fit maneuvering over a small bridge.
Courtesy of D. R. Betts, Inc., North Attleboro, Massachusetts.

visits to the town building department prior to the start of the move. Keep in mind that in the case of an old house, electrical, plumbing, and wastewater systems must be brought up to code if that has not already been completed.

2. *Utility reattachment.* All services that were disconnected at the old site must now be reconnected:

   a. *Sewer.* The public sewer will require connections and associated piping. A septic tank system will need to be designed and installed.

   b. *Water.* If water is from a public system, pipes will need to be trenched to the house. The house's distance from the system will dictate the cost. With a private water system, the well must be dug and associated piping laid.

   c. *Electricity.* Wires must be run from the existing utility poles to the house. Costs will include new poles and wires to reach the house and will vary, depending on the distance between the house and the existing lines.

 d. *Telephone.* The costs will depend on your proximity to main telephone cables.

 e. *Gas.* As with water connections, pipes will need to be trenched to
 the house, or a propane tank can be installed.

 f. *Cable television.* Similar to electricity and telephone, costs will
 depend on the distance to the main lines.

3. *New foundation.* The foundation that will support the house at the new
 site can be built prior to or after the house arrives (see chapter 7). This
 depends on the age and makeup of the house. With a typical twenty-
 four by thirty-six-foot Cape Cod home that is less than fifty years old,
 a foundation can be built prior to the arrival of the house on-site. With
 a much older house, built in a time of varying construction standards
 and little or no quality control, a new foundation should be constructed only after the house is situated over the foundation footprint.
 This way, the foundation can be precisely measured and laid out to
 accommodate any imperfections in the construction of the house.

Historic Preservation and the Federal Government's Role in Funding

What is historic preservation? According to secretary of the interior publications, historic preservation is

> the act or process of applying measures to sustain the existing form, integrity and material of a building or structure, and the existing form and vegetative cover of a site including stabilization and ongoing maintenance.

I consider historic preservation to be an attitude or a way of thinking about the conservation of structures, sites, and objects that represent a physical connection with people and events from our past. Today, historic preservation utilizes various land use planning strategies, government programs, and financial incentives to protect historic resources. The preservation of historic structures and sites helps create an inimitable environment and sense of place in cities and towns across the United States. This cultural richness strengthens the local economy by promoting tourism and encouraging investment. This, however, was not the case before the middle part of the twentieth century.

Many people believe that historic preservation in the United States began to take shape with the saving of Independence Hall in Philadelphia, Pennsylvania. Often referred to as the birthplace of our nation, Independence Hall was the site where both the Declaration of Independence and the U.S. Constitution were created. In 1816, a group of historical associations petitioned the City of Philadelphia to save the building from demolition.

Prior to the establishment of the National Trust for Historic Preservation in 1949 and the passage of the National Historic Preservation Act of 1966, the responsibility of preservation was composed of two halves: public and private. The private sector was concerned primarily with historical figures and their associated landmarks, while the public, or government, sector was focused on establishing national parks. It was not until the mid-twentieth century that preservation based on architectural significance was realized.

With the establishment of the National Historic Preservation Act of 1966, a partnership was forged between the federal government and the states, Indian tribes, local governments, private organizations, and individuals to promote the preservation of America's historic resources. Forty years later, a number of government agencies and organizations are providing support to the countless number of preservation projects throughout the United States. Federal funding for the sake of preservation is channeled into the National Park Service, the Department of Transportation, the Department of Agriculture, state and tribal historic preservation offices, certified local governments, and the Advisory Council on Historic Preservation.

RENOVATION, REHABILITATION, RESTORATION, AND RECONSTRUCTION

Often mistakenly interchangeable and thought to mean the same thing, *renovation, rehabilitation, restoration,* and *reconstruction* are all means by which an old building is brought back to life. Although difficult to distinguish from one another, each word represents an individual's mind-set on how an old building can be utilized to meet their needs:

> *Renovation.* This process is used when repairing and changing an existing building for modern use. Rather than building new, the existing building is often gutted and updated to current standards. The process may include interior and exterior changes and often requires the removal of some existing building elements.
> *Rehabilitation.* This process is used when repairing an existing building to good condition with only minor modifications to the existing fab-

ric. The secretary of the interior's *Standards for Rehabilitation*, a
guide set forth by the federal government used to undertake work
on historic buildings, defines it as follows:

> The act or process of returning a property to a state of utility through repair
> or alteration which makes possible an efficient contemporary use while pre-
> serving those portions or features of the property which are significant to
> its historical, architectural, and cultural values.

Restoration. This process is used when a building is returned to a specific period in its history. Period construction materials and methods are used to transform the building to the era of its greatest historical significance. Later additions are usually removed, and
missing period work is replaced. Restoration involves a certain
degree of speculation with respect to lost features; for it to be legiti-
mate, careful investigation and near flawless workmanship is
required.

Reconstruction. This process, seldom practiced, involves duplicating the
original materials, form, and appearance of a building no longer in
existence today. The process is difficult and expensive and may be
purely speculative.

THE NATIONAL REGISTER OF HISTORIC PLACES

Created following the establishment of the National Preservation Act of
1966, the National Register of Historic Places is the nation's official list of
structures, districts, and objects worthy of preservation because of their
importance in American history, culture, architecture, and/or archaeol-
ogy. To date, nearly 77,000 listings of over 1.2 million buildings and historic resources make up the National Register. The National Park Service,
a division of the U.S. Department of the Interior, is responsible for maintaining the program, which is administered locally through state historic
preservation offices (SHPOs). Nominations for addition to the National
Register are evaluated first by SHPO and then sent to the National Park
Service for final approval.

Nominations are based on an evaluation of properties with regard to
their historical significance at a given time. In many parts of the country,
historical commissions have compiled comprehensive inventories of their

local cultural resources to aid them in determining if a nomination is worthy of historic preservation.

Some of the principal benefits that come with a listing on the National Register are the following:

- *Recognition.* A listing on the National Register provides a property official recognition of its historic significance to local or national heritage and may increase monetary value.
- *Protection.* Properties listed on the National Register are automatically included in the State Register and are offered limited protection from adverse effects of federal and state actions, which may include demolition and relocation. Listed structures may receive special consideration or exemption from certain other regulations, such as energy conservation rules and compliance with the Americans with Disabilities Act. In addition, any changes to a listed property that involve federal funding or permitting are reviewed pursuant to section 106 of the National Historic Preservation Act. Section 106 requires federal agencies to consider the effects of their actions on historic properties and provides the Advisory Council on Historic Preservation (ACHP) an opportunity to comment on federal projects prior to implementation. As an independent federal agency, the ACHP promotes historic preservation nationally by providing a forum for influencing federal activities that impact historic preservation.
- *Tax Incentives.* The owners of income-producing properties can qualify for a tax credit for rehabilitation in accordance with standards set by the Department of the Interior and the Internal Revenue Service.
- *Grants.* Register listings owned by nonprofit organizations and municipalities are eligible, when available, for matching state grants for historic restoration.

Note that listing in the National Register does not preclude the owner's ability to alter, manage, or sell the property, as long as private funding is used.

HISTORIC DISTRICTS

A historic district is a collection of buildings recognized for their historic significance within established geographic boundaries. The collective significance of the district is often greater than the sum of its properties' individual significance. Any community can identify an unofficial district through signage and brochures. This is often done to focus attention on older neighborhood shopping areas to persuade nonlocal residents to visit and support the local economy. Official historic districts are created and sanctioned by government action and can be National Register historic districts or local historic districts.

THE NATIONAL REGISTER CRITERIA FOR LISTING

The criteria for evaluating potential entries into the National Register were designed as a guide for state and local governments, federal agencies, and preservationists dedicated to the cause of recognizing the accomplishments of persons who have made significant contributions to our country's heritage.

To list on the National Register, a property must meet at least one of the following criteria:

1. The property is associated with events that have made a significant contribution to local or national heritage.
2. The property is associated with the lives of people who have made a significant contribution to local or national heritage.
3. The property represents distinctive characteristics of type, period, or method of construction, or the collective significance of the property outweighs the individual entity.
4. The property may uncover important information in local or national prehistory or history.

The following is a list of properties that *shall not* be considered eligible for inclusion in the National Register unless they qualify as parts of a district or meet additional criteria outlined later:

1. Properties owned by religious institutions or used for religious purposes, including cemeteries.
2. Structures moved from their original locations (see the next list)
3. Historic buildings that have been reconstructed
4. Commemorative properties
5. Properties attaining significance within the past fifty years

However, these properties will qualify if they are essential components of districts that do meet the criteria or if they fall within the following categories:

1. Religious properties, including cemeteries, significant in art, architecture, historical figures, or other historical relevance
2. Structures that have been relocated and are significant in architecture or a surviving structure associated with a historic person or event (see chapter 9)
3. Reconstructed buildings part of a restoration master plan or representing a building or structure no longer in existence
4. Commemorative properties with their own exceptional significance
5. Properties attaining significance within the past fifty years that are exceptionally significant

If the consideration criteria have been fulfilled, then the next step is to contact the local historical commission or SHPO to determine if an inventory form of the property has been completed. An inventory form is a historical record of the property. The form typically contains information about the history, architecture, and archeological significance of the property. If a form has been completed, the local commission will need to be asked to forward its recommendations to the state historical commission for inclusion on the National Register. The property will then be evaluated to determine whether it meets the required criteria for listing and may be listed either individually or as part of a historic district, depending on the specific location of the property.

Once a property has met the listed criteria and is recommended by the local historical commission, the SHPO will send the home owner a nomination form and instruction manual. The form should be filled out with assistance of a professional preservation consultant and the local historical commission. Next, the completed form is submitted to your SHPO. At the SHPO, the proposed nomination is reviewed for completeness and is edited. "Intent to nominate" letters are sent to local property owners who are given the opportunity to comment on the nomination. Private property owners may agree or object to the nomination. Any response to objections on the nomination will require the help of the National Park Service at this time. If no objections are logged, the nomination is presented to the state review board for approval at the quarterly National Register meetings.

The review board is comprised of professionals in the fields of American history, architectural history, architecture, and other related disciplines. The state board will review the nomination and vote whether to nominate the property for the National Register. This takes a minimum of ninety days but will depend on the state workload and backlog. The nomination is then forwarded to the National Park Service in Washington, D.C., for final approval. A decision is then made within forty-five days on the inclusion in the National Registry of Historic Places.

RELOCATING PROPERTIES LISTED ON THE NATIONAL REGISTER

If the property is to remain listed on the National Register of Historic Places after the move, the Code of Federal Regulations must be followed. Part 60, section 60.14, of the regulations is summarized here (the complete text can be found on the National Archives and Records Administration website at www.gpoaccess.gov/cfr/ondex.html):

1. When a property is moved, every effort should be made to re-create a similar historical setting, preserving what was lost.
2. If a property is to be moved, the SHPO or federal preservation officer must submit documentation to the National Park Service prior to the move. The required documentation shall consist of the following:
   a. Reasons for the move
   b. Effects on the historical integrity of the property
   c. Proposed site specifics
   d. Photographs of proposed location
3. If a property is to be moved, proper notification procedures and approval processes must be followed. Keep in mind that if a building is located on the National Register of Historic Places, moving it may result in its removal from the Register and the loss of tax benefits.
4. If a property is moved prior to adherence to the above requirements, it is automatically deleted from the National Register.
5. Some exceptions to the above requirements may apply.

See also chapter 5.

TAX INCENTIVES, GRANTS, AND OTHER ASSISTANCE

Tax Incentives

The federal government has many programs that promote historic preservation through rehabilitation of historic and older buildings. One of these is the Federal Historic Preservation Tax Incentive Program. Since 1976, the National Park Service, in conjunction with the Internal Revenue Service and SHPOs, has administered this program that rewards property owners for investment in rehabilitating historic properties such as offices, rental housing, and retail stores. Since the program's inception, more than $25 billion has been invested in private rehabilitation, and over 29,000 historic properties have been rehabilitated.

This program provides two tax credits. A credit lowers the amount of taxes owed as opposed to a deduction, which lowers the amount of income to be taxed:

- 20 percent tax credit for the *certified rehabilitation* of *certified historic structures*
- 10 percent tax credit for the rehabilitation of nonhistoric or nonresidential buildings built before 1936

Both of these credits require a *substantial rehabilitation* and must include a *depreciable* building (see the discussion later in this chapter).

To be eligible for the 20 percent tax credit, the project must meet *all* of the following conditions set forth by the Internal Revenue Code:

1. The building to be rehabilitated must be a *certified historic structure*, that is, a building listed in the National Register of Historic Places, either on an individual basis or as a contributing property within the National Register Historic District.
2. The building must be *depreciable*. It must be used in a business or for the production of income. It can be used as rental property or offices but cannot serve exclusively as the owner's private residence.
3. The building's rehabilitation must be a "substantial rehabilitation"; that is, expenditures must equal or exceed $5,000 or the adjusted basis of the building, whichever is greater. The adjusted basis of the building is the purchase price minus the cost of the land plus improvements

already made minus depreciation already taken. To qualify, the rehabilitation can occur only within a twenty-four-month period, unless the rehabilitation is done in phases, which allots a sixty-month period. Qualified rehabilitation expenditures include costs associated with the work carried out on the historic building. These costs may include architectural and engineering fees, site survey fees, construction fees, legal expenses, and development fees. These costs do not include furnishings for the building, new additions that expand the square footage of the building, new building construction, and related facilities and landscaping, including parking lots and sidewalks.

4. The building's rehabilitation must be in accordance with federally established standards as set forth in *The Secretary of the Interior's Standards for Rehabilitation*.

The Secretary of the Interior's Standards for Rehabilitation and *Illustrated Guidelines for Rehabilitating Historic Buildings* were developed as guides for work associated with National Register properties receiving federal grants. *The Secretary of the Interior's Standards for Rehabilitation* focuses on ten principles to be followed for the rehabilitation of historic buildings. These principles emphasize repair over replacement in order to preserve those qualities for which the property is listed on the National Register. The *Illustrated Guidelines for Rehabilitating Historic Buildings* is intended to aid in applying the standards to a project. These guidelines are not project specific, and they assist owners, developers, and federal agency managers to follow, "recommended courses of action." The building's rehabilitation must be a "certified rehabilitation" as required by the Department of the Interior (see the section "Certified Rehabilitation" later in this chapter).

To be eligible for the 10 percent tax credit, the project must meet all the following conditions set forth by the Internal Revenue Code:

1. The building must be nonhistoric and built prior to 1936.
2. The building's rehabilitation must be substantial, and the property must be depreciable (see the previous discussion of the 20 percent credit).
3. The building cannot be residential; however, hotels would qualify since they are considered to be commercial.

4. The building cannot be moved; however, a certified historic structure may still be eligible for the credit.

5. The building must meet certain structural requirements as listed here:

- At least 75 percent of the building's existing walls must remain from start to finish of the rehabilitation work, 50 percent of which must be exterior walls.
- At least 75 percent of the building's internal structural framework must remain in place.

For more information on the federal historic preservation tax incentive program, visit the National Park Service website at www.cr.nps.gov/hps/tps/tax/index.htm.

Additional Funding

Not everyone can qualify for the federal government's tax credit program. Currently, the only tax incentives offered for rehabilitation of a historic building are for income-producing properties. Following is a list of alternatives, including grants, loans, and preservation funding.

The Historic Preservation Fund is administered by the National Park Service. Through yearly congressional appropriation of approximately $37 million to the Historic Preservation Fund, matching grants are provided to encourage private and nonfederal investment in historic preservation efforts nationwide. The funding can be used in a number of preservation activities, including the development of architectural plans, historic structure reports, and engineering studies necessary to repair listed properties. Additional information about this program is available on the National Park Service website at www.cr.nps.gov/helpyou.htm.

The 203(k) Mortgage Rehabilitation Insurance Program, administered by the Department of Housing and Urban Development's Federal Housing Administration, is a loan program that helps individuals buy and restore historic properties in urban or rural areas. More can be learned about this program by visiting the Housing and Urban Development website at www.hud.gov/offices/hsg/sfh/203k/faqs203k.cfm.

The National Preservation Loan Fund is administered by the National Trust and provides loans for acquisitions of rehabilitations of historic properties. For additional information about this fund, visit the National

Trust for Historic Preservation website at www.nthp.org/help/funding.-html.

The Preservation Services Fund is also run by the National Trust and offers nonprofit organizations and public agencies matching grants. Grants range from $500 to $5,000 and may be used on education, planning, or professional services, such as architectural evaluation or engineering.

Founded in 1949, the National Trust for Historic Preservation, a nonprofit organization, provides grants and loans and helps preserve the nation's historic places through its many resources, leadership, education, and advocacy. It website is www.nationaltrust.org/help/grants.html.

CERTIFIED REHABILITATION

The National Park Service (NPS) must approve those projects seeking the 20 percent rehabilitation tax credit. By approving a project, the NPS deems it a "certified historic structure," therefore certifying its rehabilitation as well. In doing so, the NPS recognizes the rehabilitation of the project as being consistent with the historic character of the district or property where it is located. The NPS assumes that the historic building may be altered to provide for an efficient use; however, these alterations must not damage, destroy, or cover interior or exterior features that help define the character of the building.

Steps involved in helping to get your project approved or certified are listed here:

1. Consult with the SHPO and apply as soon as possible. Study the program application and regulations along with any other information supplied by the SHPO. Submit the application as early in the project planning process as possible and wait for notification in writing by the NPS before beginning work. Work started prior to approval by the NPS may jeopardize certification.
2. Proper documentation using before and after photographs the projects is crucial. "Before" photographs are particularly essential. Without them, it may be impossible for the NPS to approve your project.
3. Read and follow *The Secretary of the Interior's Standards for Rehabilitation* and the *Illustrated Guidelines for Rehabilitating Historic Buildings*.

4. Notify the SHPO and the NPS of any changes to the scope of work that occur after you have applied for certification.

HIRING A HISTORIC PRESERVATION CONSULTANT

An experienced historic preservation consultant can manage a historic building's research efforts, acknowledgment (National Register), tax advantages, and even funding appropriation, helping to facilitate the entire project (see also chapter 5).

Historic preservation consultants can assist a project in many different ways. There are various types of preservation consultants, including archeologists, historians, preservation architects, and planners and engineers. These various professionals, who have the education and experience, often work as a team with the home owner to help guide the project to its successful completion.

Often with a historic building, historic preservation consultants can be called on to prepare a "historic structures report." Such a report is a comprehensive description of the building with respect to its history, form and fabric, existing conditions, required repairs, and priorities for those repairs.

With this information in hand, the project can proceed on the basis of knowledge and rationale rather than momentum, impulse, and, all too often, uninformed panic. Hiring an appropriate historic preservation consultant will improve the quality of your project, save time and money, and help protect the historic property.

5

Historic House Moving

A historic house is more than just an old structure; it is a discernible link allowing us the opportunity to view and be a part of the past. Such a house gives communities a sense of identity and belonging in the fabric that helped build this country. This chapter discusses the additional steps required in the moving of a historic house.

Daniel Webster, one of the greatest spokesmen for American nationalism, owned many houses, three of which were in Portsmouth, New

FIGURE 5.1
The Daniel Webster House at Strawbery Banke in Portsmouth, New Hampshire.
Courtesy of the author.

Hampshire. One house was burned, the other fell victim to urban renewal, and the third, shown in figure 5.1 originally built on High Street in 1785, was moved in 1961 to the Strawbery Banke National Historic District site. The house is distinguished by its fascinating roof, which has one gable end, one hip end, and wide eaves.

PRESERVATION THROUGH RELOCATION

Starting in the late 1980s, continuing through the 1990s, and now more than ever, a convergence of lifestyle and a booming economy has dramatically increased the number of older homes being demolished. The practice, commonly referred to as "teardown," typically affects attractive historic neighborhoods in close proximity to metropolitan areas. Older homes are razed, making way for much larger houses in their place. The final product is an enormous house shoehorned into place without regard for the scale or character of the neighborhood.

Rather than tearing down the house, one alternative is to move it. Relocation preserves a building; however, its historic relationship with the site is lost. Moving a historic building should not be undertaken lightly. It should be considered only after all other alternatives, such as renovation, rehabilitation, and expansion, have been exhausted. It is only under very limited circumstances, such as demolition, that a building should be subjected to the stresses of being moved.

For example, a historically significant building threatened with demolition or surrounded by an environment incompatible with an adoptive use can be relocated to a more compatible site. This, as part of a revitalization plan, can result in several benefits: saving the building, enhancing the environment, and possibly increasing the value of the real estate. Remember, the value of a historic house is figured not solely on the makeup of the house but also on its surroundings. Although moving it compromises its historic integrity, setting, and environment, the benefits can sometimes outweigh the disadvantages.

The Goodwin Mansion (figure 5.2) was constructed in 1811 on upper Islington Street, across from Goodwin Park, an upscale section of Portsmouth at the time. The house's flat facade and neoclassical columns typifies the Federal architectural style. Designed by architect Charles Bullfinch, the style of the house was influenced by the British architect Robert Adam and by neoclassicism in general.

The house was home to one of Portsmouth's most influential men in

Portsmouth. N. H.
Gov. Goodwin Mansion erected 1811,
Islington Street.
Home of First War Governor of
New Hampshire.

FIGURE 5.2
The Governor Goodwin Mansion in 1812 on Islington Street in Portsmouth,
New Hampshire.
Courtesy of the Portsmouth Public Library.

the nineteenth century. Governor Ichabod Goodwin, the state's first Civil
War governor, and his wife, Sarah Parker, lived in the house. In addition
to being elected governor in 1859 and 1860, Ichabod was a state representative for many years. He went on to serve as the president of two banks,
the Portsmouth Bridge Company, the Portsmouth Steam Factory, the
Portsmouth Gas Company, the Eastern Railroad, and the Portsmouth
Whaling Company.

Facing demolition for the use of the land it occupied, the Goodwin
Mansion was moved to Strawbery Banke in 1963 as one of the few buildings moved primarily for its historic significance.

The house was cut into two main sections plus three smaller top sections. It was first moved across the street into Goodwin Park. Next it was
moved down Islington Street to Newton Avenue, where it was set on cribbing before traveling to its final destination at Strawbery Banke (figure
5.3).

The Goodwin Mansion relocation illustrates the importance of topo-
graphical setting and context consistent with the original site of the building. Icabod's wife, Sarah, was an avid gardener and kept an extensive jour-

FIGURE 5.3
The Governor Goodwin Mansion in 2003 on Hancock Street at Strawbery Banke in
Portsmouth, New Hampshire.
Courtesy of the author.

nal recording plant varieties, dates of bloom, and favorite plant
combinations. The journal also described the wonderful views she had of
the garden from the window of the house that overlooked it. After the
house was moved, the garden was re-created through an 1862 garden plan
and the journals written by Mrs. Goodwin. To someone unfamiliar with
the original site, its re-creation may seem fairly accurate; however, to
someone like Mrs. Goodwin, it is likely that the wonderful view she had
grown accustomed to could never be re-created.

SELECTING THE NEW SITE
The integrity and significance of a historic house go hand in hand with its
surrounding landscape. When a house is removed from its original location, a portion of its heritage is lost. In addition, the heritage of the landscape from which it was removed is altered forever. Most important, if the
house is listed on the National Register, it is crucial to its continued listing
and status to be located on a property as much like the original as possible.

Every effort should be made to reestablish the historic orientation and landscape features of the relocated structure at its new site.

The selection of a new site takes careful and thorough planning and may require the expertise of an architect and historic landscape planner. It is important that setting and location with respect to light and shadow enhance rather than detract from the aesthetic quality of a structure. In addition, the selection of the new site should consider adjacent buildings and their relationship to the relocated structure. Particular attention should be paid to mass and shape. A relocated structure that is not proportional in size or shape with surrounding buildings may appear awkward or out of place, adversely affecting the historical significance of an area.

The Pope-Leighey House is a perfect example of the importance of context and intended setting. The house, commissioned in 1939, was designed by Frank Lloyd Wright. As a dwelling for people of moderate means, the house represents Wright's Usonian period and the trends in American home design following World War II.

FIGURE 5.4
Frank Lloyd Wright's Pope-Leighey House in Falls Church, Virginia, in 1963.
Courtesy of the National Trust for Historic Preservation.

The 1,200-square-foot house was built in 1940–1941 at a cost of $7,000, including land and built-in furniture. Its revolutionary design included cantilevered flat roofs, a combined living/dining area, the first covered carport, and unity between interior and exterior space. Other innovations included radiant-heated slab-on-grade flooring and board-and-batten wall surfaces, a type of wood-siding construction whereby wide vertical boards are covered at the joints by narrow boards, both inside and out, creating studless walls.

The Leigheys lived in the house from 1946 through the early 1960s. In 1963, Mrs. Leighey received a final notice of intent from the state regarding the realignment of Interstate 66 and the destruction of her house. She then arranged a deal to donate the house to the Trust for Historic Preservation in conjunction with the National Park Service. The state paid her a $31,500 dislocation allowance based on the value of her home.

In 1964, the house was moved sixteen miles from its original location

FIGURE 5.5
Frank Lloyd Wright's Pope-Leighey House in Mount Vernon, Virginia, in 1964.
Courtesy of the National Trust for Historic Preservation.

to the National Trust's Woodlawn Plantation in Alexandria, Virginia. As with any house designed by Frank Lloyd Wright, the relationship between the house and its surrounding landscape was of paramount importance. The site was chosen for the natural topography, landscaping, and seclusion from public roadways. Under the supervision of master carpenter Howard C. Rickert, the original builder, the house was partially disassembled, moved, and then reassembled at the new site. Over time, the house began to exhibit substantial settlement cracking because of poor soil conditions and thus had to be moved again a short distance in 1995.

At this new site, the issue was no longer the soil conditions but rather the poor placement of the house with respect to its surroundings. A firm was hired by the National Trust for Historic Preservation to evaluate the condition of the structure, its surroundings, and future location.

It was decided that the house would again be dismantled and moved seventy-five feet uphill, where it would be reassembled and restored to its

FIGURE 5.6
The Pope-Leighey House in Mount Vernon, Virginia, in 2000.
Courtesy of Peter Beers.

original grandeur. Here it still sits today as testament to preservation and dexterous relocation.

THE NEW FOUNDATION

The continued preservation of the structure at its new site depends in part on its foundation. The purpose of the foundation is to support the structure and keep water and insects from causing deterioration. Although the new foundation should take advantage of modern design and construction methods, keeping the historic significance of the structure intact should be of utmost importance.

If a full or partial basement is a requirement, then typically a new foundation will consist of reinforced-concrete walls and slab with the appropriate waterproofing material used to maintain a dry basement. The type of waterproofing used is dictated by the type of drainage used and the presence of a water table.

Regardless of the type of modern materials used in providing a moisture-resistant foundation, the visible exterior and interior faces of the foundation can be covered by the original fascia material, such as brick, fieldstone, or dressed stone. This is achieved by photographing and measuring the fascia materials at the existing site to accurately depict the visible portion of the foundation above finished grade at the new site. On the interior, if the finished basement will be used as a potential exhibit area, then the entire face of the wall should be covered with the appropriate original fascia material. With this approach, the historic texture of the walls is preserved and visible, while the modern techniques in stability and water impermeability are camouflaged.

If the basement space is deemed critical to the interpretive nature of the restored structure, then the basement walls that make up the foundation must be dismantled and moved to the new site. This is achieved by photographing, measuring, and marking the various pieces of the foundation to reassemble them like puzzle pieces. Marking and transporting the pieces of the foundation can be done in a variety of ways. It is recommended that a structural mover experienced in historic building relocations be used. Such a mover should have the appropriate resources on hand or have the knowledge of where to find individuals with experience in dismantling and reassembling stone or masonry structures.

CONSIDERATIONS PRIOR TO THE MOVE

After the selection of the structural mover, the next step is to perform a condition assessment of the exterior and interior of the house. The structural mover and (usually) the town building inspector will evaluate the house to determine if it is structurally sound for the relocation process. The home owner's job or that of the project preservation consultant, architect, structural engineer, or restoration specialist is to conduct an initial conservation analysis to determine areas that may develop into extensive restoration difficulties. Such problems may include insect infestation, rot, or water damage.

Along with the condition survey, thorough documentation and recordings of the move and restoration of the property should be performed. Certain precautions can be taken to protect important structural and architectural features and to ensure compatibility of the historic building in its new location. The following recommendations can be used as a guide for documentation prior to relocating the structure:

1. *Photographic documentation.* Create a set of photo plans. Photo plans are a set of drawings similar to the set of measured drawings but contain a series of numbers or letters used to identify a specific photograph and the direction in which it was taken. The photographs can be symbolized by a circle and arrow pointing in the direction that the picture was taken. If one were to stand at that point and look in the direction of the arrow, that is what would be seen. This type of symbolism can be used on the site plan, floor plans, and details.

    Photograph the present appearance of the building on the inside and outside. Inside, pay particular attention to structural elements, decorative trim, wall or ceiling finishes, mantels, and staircases. These types of elements are often compromised if the house is partially or totally disassembled for relocation. Outside, photograph all sides of the structure, including adjacent buildings and landscape; doors and windows; masonry features, such as chimneys; and roof elements, such as slate shingles.

2. *Notes.* It may be true that a picture is worth a thousand words, but I would not want to commit all those details to memory. Rather, I strongly recommend writing them all down or recording them on a tape recorder and then transcribing them. Take as many notes as possi-

ble and use the photographs to complete the picture. If the house is to be dismantled and put back together, thorough documentation consisting of numerous photographs and associated text will make the reassembly accurate and much easier to complete.

3. *Dimensional drawings.* Typically, dimensional or measured drawings can be prepared by an engineer, architect, or skilled draftsperson. A complete set of drawings should include the following:

   a. *Site plan.* A drawing that depicts walls, walkways, gardens, trees, shrubs, and outbuildings. It should also include some spot elevations to get a sense of the topography of the site.

   b. *Floor plans.* Drawings that illustrate the layout of each of the levels in the house, including basement, ground floor, first floor, and attic.

   c. *Framing plans.* Drawings that represent the sizes of the structural elements, including beams and columns.

   d. *Elevations.* Drawings that illustrate the faces of the house of both interior and exterior walls with all features shown as if in a single vertical plane.

   e. *Sections.* Drawings that illustrate the view of a house if it were cut vertically and the interior exposed. Sections should taken through various parts of the building, including decorative trim details and molding profiles.

   f. *Details.* Drawings that depict a portion of the structure, such as a structural connection.

After completing all the required documentation, consider submitting the information to the local historical commission. This information may be used in producing future inventory forms of the property. Used in preservation planning, inventory forms are documents kept by local historical commissions that identify and describe significant buildings and structures in the town. A significant building or structure may reflect distinctive features of the architectural, cultural, economic, political, or social history of the town.

PREPARING THE STRUCTURE FOR THE MOVE

Depending on the method your structural mover chooses (see chapter 6), some of the key elements to a successful project are strengthening the structure for the move, protecting it during the move, and providing concise markings to partially or fully reconstruct the house after the move (see chapter 7).

If the house is to be moved intact, critical repairs may be made to main load-bearing members, wall-framing elements, and sills prior to moving day. Depending on the severity of the deteriorated elements, the potential for damage to the historic fabric of the structure, or time constraints at the existing site, temporary repairs may be made to allow the structure to travel to its new location, where extensive restoration can then take place. In many cases, timber members can be temporarily attached to structurally sound elements to transfer the loads of the structure over deteriorated sections.

To protect the structure during the move, plywood is nailed to the exterior window frames to protect the window glass, and masonry chimneys are stabilized with bracing elements or removed, as required in some parts of the country.

When moving a partially disassembled structure, plywood sheets and/or nylon tarps are used to temporarily cover exposed areas that were previously protected by the roof or side walls. These materials not only protect against inclement weather but also guard against vandals and are removed as the house is reassembled.

With stacked timber in place to act as rails for the dollies to travel over, the house will be pulled over the new foundation, which will be built up to meet the underside of the house.

Historic New England, formerly the Society for the Preservation of New England Antiquities (SPNEA), is an organization that protects the architectural and cultural heritage of New England. Founded in 1910, SPNEA's mission is to provide the public with an insightful understanding of the history of New England life through its substantial collection of buildings, landscapes, and objects dating from the seventeenth century to the present.

The Alexander House was constructed sometime between 1811 and 1812. Its design is attributed to the work of Asher Benjamin, specifically his 1806 book titled *The American Builder's Companion*. Working as a carpenter for most of his life, Benjamin wrote seven handbooks or builders' guides compiling his life experience specifically to aid the American builder. At the time, these books served as the only architectural reference guides for carpenters and builders throughout New England.

FIGURE 5.7
Alexander House, Springfield, Massachusetts (1811).
Courtesy of Historic New England, formerly the Society for the Preservation of New England
Antiquities.

The Alexander House is a wonderful example of the transition from the
Federal style of architecture to the Greek Revival domestic architecture
built in New England between 1810 and 1820. Because of its popularity, it
became known as the National style.

Owners of the house included the postmaster of Springfield, a colonel
who played a role in the Louisiana Purchase and a well-known artist
whose portraits of Daniel Webster currently hang in the Cincinnati Art
Museum. After several modifications and one 200-foot relocation, ownership of the house was finally conveyed to SPNEA in 1939.

During its ownership, SPNEA leased portions of the house for office
and residential space until 1993, after which the house remained vacant.
In 2003, when the U.S. General Services Administration proposed that a
new federal courthouse be built on the site, the house was moved to a
neighboring historic district in town.

With the house now at its new location, SPNEA will sell the house with
perpetual preservation restrictions, a partnership between the property
owner and SPNEA with a shared goal of protecting the historic character
of the house indefinitely.

6

Choosing a Method for Moving

The success of the project will in large part be attributed to the choice in the type of move. Houses can be moved in three conditions: intact or one piece, completely disassembled, or partially disassembled. The structural mover will take several factors into consideration in making this decision:

1. *Structural integrity.* The mover must determine the structural integrity of the building by examining the main load-bearing elements for any degree of deterioration. Main elements include sills, main beams, walls, and roof elements. Depending on the level of deterioration, if any, several repair options can be investigated, including extensive structural bracing, partial or complete dismantling and replacement, and then replacing decayed elements on reassembling the structure.

2. *Construction material.* A timber structure is by far the easiest to move and provides a variety of options in the method of relocation. Masonry, such as brick or cement masonry units, typically increases costs primarily because of the weight of the structure, clearance issues with height, and weight restrictions on both roads and bridges. Sometimes masonry structures can be partially disassembled. Removing the roof and any components attached to the main house can increase moving options.

3. *Surrounding landscape.* The landscape surrounding the structure to be moved can largely affect the method selected. For example, if the structure is built into a hillside, getting it to a higher or lower elevation can be so costly in labor and materials that this task alone could far exceed the entire

project budget. In this case, it would be wise to consider partial or total disassembly.

4. *Relocation route.* The route in which a house travels toward its final destination can be full of obstacles. In some instances, avoiding these obstacles will limit your options on the method of moving. Under ideal conditions, the house being moved is of timber construction, small enough to travel below utility lines, and narrow enough to avoid curbs, signs, fences, and the like.

MOVING IN ONE PIECE

Whenever possible, it is recommended that a building be moved in one piece. Of the three methods, this one ensures the least amount of damage to the historic fabric of the structure. Although this method may make economic sense by eliminating the need for dismantling and reassembly of the structure, sometimes the utility costs of raising, lowering, or temporarily removing wires may be cost prohibitive to the project (see chapter 8).

If the age and physical condition of the structure are in question or the relocation route precludes moving the structure as a single unit, then partial disassembly into smaller sections may be your option. It is only under extreme conditions that a structure be totally disassembled.

The house in figure 6.1 was moved back from the eroding shoreline. Since it remained on its existing lot, it was advantageous for scheduling and economic reasons that the house be moved intact.

TOTAL DISASSEMBLY

When a house is totally disassembled, all parts that make up the structure, including clapboards, sheathing, chimney, framing elements, floorboards, windows, doors, and finish work, are removed and cataloged. Why disassemble a house?

One way to save a home on an endangered list that is threatened with demolition is to dismantle and store it for future reassembly by a prospective buyer. Not all houses on these lists are saved. What sets some apart are their age and historic significance. Houses built in colonial times possess features not often found in homes built today. These may include post-and-beam construction with hand-hewn logs and wood pegs used to interlock joints, large decorated brickwork chimneys, hand-carved wood-

FIGURE 6.1
House being moved intact.
Courtesy of Hayden Building Movers, Cotuit, Massachusetts.

work, and original hardware. Houses such as these set for demolition are prime candidates to be saved.

Throughout the country, companies that call themselves "preservationists" may in fact be "preservationists based on a profit margin." These companies buy old homes, dismantle them, and ship them to high-end clienteles for profit. The majority of these historic structures are in fact threatened to be destroyed, but some are dismantled and sold purely for profit.

One advantage to dismantling a house, at least from an architectural historian's view, is the ability to witness the evolution of the structure over its useful life. As each layer of the structure is pulled away, a genealogy of the house can be examined and documented in detail. Every layer of wallpaper represents a different decorative style and taste but, more important, a link to a specific time in history—the essence of preservation.

When a house is completely disassembled, many elements original to the house are lost in the process. For example, clay or lime mortars used in the joints between fieldstone foundation walls and chimney linings will be lost. Over time, elements such as clapboards and exterior sheathing can become brittle and often are destroyed in the process of removal. Frame elements typically held together by wooden pegs can fracture when disengaged from supporting elements because of the age of the timber members. Removal of interior finish work requires advanced carpentry skills. Amateur dismantling quite often results in irreparable damage.

The dismantling of a house usually takes more than one individual; therefore, it is important to establish certain guidelines and project standards prior to the commencement of the dismantling phase. The structure's original orientation with respect to compass points should be established and used by all personnel responsible for dismantling and reassembling the house. A simple marking code should also be established for the project, including the types of writing implements used in marking pieces of the house. The types of implements should not wash off easily or be permanent but should be removable with some degree of applied pressure; of course, any marking must avoid damage to the piece or be hidden from final reassembly. The use of a single color or a consistent pattern on an area will ensure the identification of all the required pieces at that specific location when reassembled. A simple yet ingenious mark-

FIGURE 6.2
House being totally disassembled south of Manchester, Vermont.
Courtesy of the author.

ing is a bold line drawn across any sheathed surface, such as pieces of adjoining plywood or lath, to ensure the correct fit during the reassembly phase.

For large masonry units existing in walls, foundations, or chimneys, successive numbering on the top surface of the element should be employed for the proper reassembling of the structure. These marks will be hidden by the next course. For smaller bricks that would require the tedious task of cleaning and numbering thousands of individual units, an option may be to break the walls into large manageable sections at the joints or to completely disassemble the bricks and reconstruct them using a reproduction of the original mortar.

The order of the dismantling process is crucial to the stability and historical integrity of the structure (see also chapter 5). First, the interior is thoroughly documented by an archivist who labels every floorboard, window, door, and even chair rail as to its orientation and location in relation to a fixed point. A photographic plan is then created, and a set of drawings is created to aid in the reconstruction of the house.

The dismantling process begins with the removal of all interior elements. Depending on the degree of preservation, moldings, wainscoting, plaster and lath, doors, windows, and floors are marked, removed, de-nailed, and packaged for reassembly.

If an interior wall is embellished with a painting or other decoration, preserving the original fabric of the particular room of the house should be of paramount importance. In this case, the structural supports that frame the wall to the rest of the house should be considered inferior to what is on the wall. The portion of the wall containing the painting or mural should be cut away from the rest of the structure while maintaining structural integrity after its removal.

Once all items within the house that are able to be preserved are removed, the skin and frame of the house are left. This typically consist of roofing boards, sheathing, shingles, clapboards, attic floorboards, roof beams, columns, floor beams, and wall studs. As these elements are being removed, a constant bracing and monitoring of the house's structural integrity should be observed. The frame should then be covered with tarps to keep out the weather and prepare for dismantling. In addition, any missing or broken elements are noted and included in the reassembly drawings. After the framing pieces are labeled and numbered for reassembly, the frame is ready to be taken apart. Any wooden pegs or pins holding the frame in place should be systematically removed. All attempts should be made to avoid drilling or cutting them loose since this would damage the original fabric of the structure. Although framing elements can be massive and heavy, they can also be brittle and dry, causing them to crack or shatter on sudden impact. Particular care should be taken during removal and transportation. Once the structure is completely disassembled, the frame and associated elements of the house are sent to their final destination or to storage for future reassembly.

PARTIAL DISASSEMBLY

Cutting a house into smaller workable pieces to make it easier to transport constitutes a partial disassembly. Determining where to cut poses a small challenge. The idea is to cut the structure in such a way that there is minimal damage to interior and exterior elements, particularly if the house is historic, yet cutting in a way that will allow the structure to be moved easily without compromising its structural integrity.

Because of the size of the house, its relation to adjacent structures, a

FIGURE 6.3
A house being moved partially disassembled.
Courtesy of the author.

FIGURE 6.4
A house being reassembled at the new site.
Courtesy of Joy Marks, Nantucket, Massachusetts.

lack of travel route options, the narrowness of certain streets, and utility interferences on the island of Nantucket, the house shown in figure 6.3 was cut into five major sections in order to facilitate its move. With the first three sections of the house in place, one of two remaining pieces is lifted into position (figure 6.4).

By looking at the exterior of a house, the structural mover usually can identify locations for possible cuts. Primary candidates for cutting are usually additions to the main house, such as porches, decks, porticoes, or protruding bay windows. The structural mover's goal is to remove portions of the house that will require the least amount of work to support during the relocation and reattach once the structure is in place. Temporary structural bracing is used to prevent racking or swaying of the structure during the raising and moving phases. As portions are removed, elements once supported by a common wall are now required to be borne on temporary shoring.

In some cases, the mover has no alternative but to cut the main house. Here, time and labor costs will increase, and the risk of a compromise to original elements will be greater, but the overall potential for irreparable damage is reduced.

As with total disassembly, maneuvering large pieces of a house around and onto trailers will require the use of a crane. This can be expensive, but in the end, this approach may in fact turn out to decrease the overall project cost, particularly in terms of labor costs during the reassembly stage.

7

The Structural Mover's Role

Although the process of moving a house may seem overwhelming, the actual physical move of a house, left to the professional structural mover, can be relatively easy. From the initial site consultation and subsequent visits to the existing and future site, the structural mover can prepare a systematic plan for moving the house. The relocation process can be broken down into four phases: preparation, lifting, moving, and setting down. To accomplish phases expeditiously and safely, many variables must be considered. Depending on the size and makeup of the house, be it timber or masonry construction, the soil and foundation types at both sites, the transportation route, and the number of pieces in which the house will be transported, the structural mover will determine how to best execute the house move.

To help the home owner gain an appreciation for the art of moving houses, this chapter briefly describes some of the tools that a structural mover may use and their functions.

THE TOOLS OF A STRUCTURAL MOVER

Movers in the business for a number of years have acquired many tools to aid them in a variety of tasks. If the mover does not possess a tool, sometimes he will make it. It is not uncommon for a mover to construct a tool to fit a unique situation. Most of the time, the result saves the mover valuable time and effort, translating into possible savings for the home owner. The following sections list the most commonly used tools and their functions.

Block Timbers or Cribbing

An essential tool to all structural movers is block timbers. Block timbers, also known as cribbing or blocking, are used as foundations supporting the heavy jack loads and distributing them to the soil below. Cribbing is made from hemlock, spruce, or oak timber. Oak is a very hard wood, with a high resistance to crushing, and is used primarily when lifting a masonry building. Hemlock, the preferred choice of a structural mover, is less expensive and moderately strong and is sometimes used as a substitute for oak. These timbers can range from four by four inches to eight by eight inches in a variety of lengths, most commonly four feet. Cribbing stacks are formed by aligning these timbers in tiers that run in alternate directions.

Jacks and the Unified™ Jacking Machine

A jack is a mechanism by which an object is raised or lowered. There are a variety of jacks that are used for lifting purposes. One of the first types of jacks to be used was a screw jack. A screw jack, or house jack, is comprised of a large screw threaded into a sleeve that widens at the base. Atop the screw sits a flat collar that provides a lifting surface. A steel turning bar is inserted into a hole through the top of the screw and turned to raise or lower the screw. The lifting process when using a screw jack is often slow and hard. As the height of the lift increases, so does the force required to turn the screw.

The use of hydraulic jacks has made the lifting process faster and less wearisome. The most common hydraulic jack is the crib jack. The crib jack consists of a base and a jacking cylinder that houses a piston of a specified diameter that extends to a given height. The jack has grooves along its length that enable it to become locked into the base at different heights. Hydraulic fluid is pumped into the cavity within the cylinder below the piston at a given pressure; as the cavity is filled, the piston rises.

The Unified™ Jacking Machine (UJM) has replaced the screw jack in most current house moves. This machine uniformly raises and lowers a series of jacks, each connected independently via hydraulic hoses to the manifold of the UJM.

Rollers

Rollers provide the ability to move the structure laterally. Rollers began as rounded timbers on which the structure rested while being pushed or pulled. In time, movers transitioned from rounded timbers to lead pipes and ultimately to "rollers." Rollers come in all different shapes and sizes.

A roller, or "skate" as they are sometimes called, is comprised of a series of steel cylinders (one inch in diameter and three inches long) encased in a housing box (figure 7.1).

Moving Dollies

In essence, moving dollies are a series of truck axles. These dollies are most likely what the house will travel on once the house is lifted off its foundation, unless a trailer or rollers on beams are used to transport it. Dollies consist of two sets of four wheels, a lifting tab or base where the load rests, and a hitch from which the dolly can be pulled or where additional dollies can be connected.

Several dollies can be connected to accommodate larger loads as pictured in figure 7.2. If the move requires use of a bridge, viaduct, or culvert, the number of dollies needed is often dictated by the state department of transportation (DOT). The DOT is responsible for the maintenance of all bridges and highways within its respective state.

The DOT lists weight restrictions for facilities under its jurisdiction. Structures designed for vehicular traffic are built to a specific maximum axle load. If this load is exceeded, the structure could become unstable or even collapse. Using several sets of dollies allows the load to be distributed over more axles, thus reducing the individual axle load to within acceptable limits.

Lifting Beams

Lifting beams are either steel I beams or timber. "I beam" refers to an iron or a steel beam with a symmetrical I-shaped cross section. These

FIGURE 7.1
A roller or skate.
Courtesy of Hevi-Haul International, Ltd.

FIGURE 7.2
Dollies grouped together.
Courtesy of Ron Holland House Moving, Inc.

beams may be in direct contact with the structure or under timber that supports the structure. Lifting beams are supported on jacks that in turn are supported on cribbing that rests on the ground. The number of lifting beams required will depend on the size and makeup of the house.

The lot move depicted in figure 7.3 entailed lifting the combined masonry and timber-frame house off its existing foundation and rolling it farther back on the lot. The difference in elevation from the original foundation to the final location at the back of the property was approximately eighteen feet. Note the stacks of cribbing leading to the location of the new foundation.

TIMBER FRAMING

With timber construction, the structure is framed primarily with wood members consisting of *posts*, *studs*, *girts*, *girders*, *floor joists*, and *rafters*. There are several different types of wood-frame construction methods, depending on time period and geographical location, but some of the most common are listed here.

FIGURE 7.3
Seven lifting beams run front to back, and two main lifting beams run across the
width of the house.
Courtesy of D. R. Betts, Inc., North Attleboro, Massachusetts.

1. *Timber frame, or post and beam.* The most common type of house
   framing in North America from around 1600 to 1800 utilized primarily
   vertical elements, such as columns and posts, supporting beams, and
   rafters. Framing was held together through the use of mortise-and-
   tenon joinery, which entailed cutting a pocket into a frame member
   that would receive the projecting end of another member. Once the
   pieces are joined, a hole is drilled at their intersection, and a wooden
   peg is inserted to draw the timber members tight and keep them
   together.
2. *Balloon, or braced, frame.* This framing system, used in Chicago in the
   1830s, is comprised entirely of two-by members. All vertical members,
   such as corner posts and studs, run uninterrupted from sill plates at
   the foundation level to the roof plates. Ledger beams attached to the
   continuous studs help support the floor joists at intermediate levels.
   Wind and earthquake loads are absorbed and transferred through the

diagonal bracing. By the twentieth century, the balloon frame was replaced by the platform frame.

3. *Platform frame.* This framing scheme became the most widely used after World War II and replaced the balloon frame. The framing system consists of a platform made up of header beams, joists, and the rough flooring at each level. Stud walls run from the sole plates, which are attached to the rough flooring, to the girts in the floor above. In this fashion, the loads are transferred from the studs to the main girders and headers and ultimately to the corner posts.

After verifying the type of framing scheme, the mover can then get a better idea of the weight of the structure and how loads are transferred through the structure and into the foundation. Taking into account the width, the number of stories, and if a center-bearing wall exists in the house, a determination of the size and placement of the lifting and transport beams can then be made, as can judgments on where cuts can be made for a partial disassembly and where additional bracing may be required to support the house.

MASONRY CONSTRUCTION

In masonry construction, stone, brick, or cement masonry units are stacked, one unit bearing on the one below, with mortar typically between the units to act as bonding agent. Masonry walls can be either *veneer* or *load bearing*. In veneered walls, the masonry exists simply as a weather barrier and ornamental facade. The wall is attached but not bonded to the supporting structure and does not carry any load. In load-bearing walls, the masonry acts a primary supporting element and can be designed to support imposed loads, such as floor or roof loading.

Unlike timber, which allows for slight flexibility from unanticipated loads imposed on the structure during a move, masonry must remain rigid at all times. When loads are applied to masonry, causing bending, cracking may occur at the mortared joints between the units. Unless the structure is properly braced, damage will most likely occur.

Masonry also tends to become brittle with age and can be quite difficult to move without the proper support. Depending on the severity of the deteriorated brick, different types of banding methods can be used to keep the brick intact. Banding is a way of wrapping the brick units, forcing them to compress and therefore stay intact. One method of banding uses pieces of timber placed against the brick at various locations. Steel cables are then wrapped around the structure against the timber pieces. Another way is to construct a frame of steel or timber against the exterior corners of the building to provide additional reinforcement of the brick.

SOIL CONDITIONS

An important aspect of a move is the type of soil at both the existing and the new site. Knowing the composition of the soil at both sites, the structural mover can choose the types of equipment used in excavating and transporting the house.

If the soil is sandy, such as that found at the beach, or muddy, additional preparations must be undertaken to ensure that the house will be raised and transported safely. Sandy or muddy soil is very unstable and shifts when a load is applied to it. The route the house travels over will then need to be stiffened in order to support the weight of the house once off its foundation.

If the house is moved in winter, the sand or soil may be frozen, and the additional cost of stabilization may be avoided. If, however, poor soil conditions are encountered, the most common solution is cribbing, plywood, or both. Depending on the weight of the house and associated support framing, cribbing can be placed side by side to act as a solid travel surface. This may be ideal when the travel distance is short. A long distance could exhaust the mover's entire supply of cribbing or could require that each piece be picked up, moved, and reset at the front of the line once the dollies and moving vehicles have passed over them.

Plywood three-quarters to one inch thick can also be used as temporary roadway over unstable soil. Sometimes plywood and cribbing are used in combination to increase the capacity of the travel surface or to reduce the amount of cribbing used. For much larger loading, such as a masonry structure, steel plates and other engineered products can be used to facilitate the heavier axle loads. In any case, the cost will be relayed to the home owner.

There are usually strict requirements when moving a house off of or along a beach. A move along a beach can be denied because it disrupts beach accessibility. Permission must be obtained from all owners of beachfront property that the structure crosses, and any voids in the sand left when a house is removed must be filled with native sand. In addition, a move along a beach might be denied if it is considered adverse to the bird population. In many parts of the country, plovers and terns, aquatic birds that nest in dunes, are considered endangered, and disturbing these birds or their eggs can carry substantial fines.

Soils containing large amounts of clay present a similar challenge. Clay soils are stiffer than sandy soils but are difficult to excavate and tend to settle over time when a load is applied.

The presence of a high groundwater table or tides can also complicate a move. One option may be to carry out the move when the water table or tide is at its lowest point. This option, however, may not fit into the timetable set by either the town or the mover.

If rock is encountered, just excavating around the foundation could deplete your entire budget. This should be discovered by a veteran structural mover and brought to your attention before the contract to move the house is even signed. Signs that may point to possible dealings with rock are rock outcroppings, rock viable at the surface of a site, rocky soils, or mountainous terrain.

FOUNDATIONS

The foundation of a house connects the house frame to the ground. The objective of the foundation is to distribute the vertical loads of the structure directly to the soil and to secure the frame of the house against wind and earthquake loads.

A properly constructed foundation keeps out moisture, insulates against the cold, and stabilizes the surrounding soil. Taking advantage of the latest materials and techniques will extend the life of your foundation for decades to come. If the foundation is to be newly constructed rather than moved from the original site for historic purposes, then the material of choice is reinforced concrete.

Foundation types can vary, depending on where you live in the United States. The three most common are basements, crawl spaces, and slab on grade.

1. *Basement.* An area below the first floor, usually between heights of six to seven feet, having foundation walls composed of fieldstone, cast-in-place concrete, or concrete masonry units.

- *Fieldstone.* A type of construction common for foundation walls constructed up until the early to mid-twentieth century. These walls consist of stones of varying sizes and shapes, tightly stacked with or without mortar.
- *Cast-in-place concrete.* A mixture of cement and coarse and fine aggregate that may include pebbles, crushed stone, brick, sand, and water in specific proportions. Forms are erected, and the concrete mixture is then poured into them. After the concrete has set or hardened, the forms are removed.
- *Concrete masonry units (CMU).* A prefabricated structural component, also referred to as concrete block, that is composed of concrete and ranges in size from a brick to a concrete block measuring eight by twelve by sixteen inches.

2. *Crawl space.* An uninhabitable area between the soil and the first floor extending below the frost line, or four feet deep. Crawl spaces may be constructed with foundation walls and footings or, if above grade, through the use of piers, which are columns that provide supplementary support to prevent the overspanning of beams and girders.

3. *Slab on grade.* A concrete floor or slab that is poured directly on the ground and acts as the first-floor subsurface. The slab is usually supported by a continuous spread footing, which is a concrete pad usually sixteen to twenty-four inches wide and six to sixteen inches deep found around the entire perimeter of the slab.

Depending on the makeup of the existing foundation and the one at the new site, the structural mover can lay out the support structure that will lift the house, transport it, and lower it onto the new foundation.

PREPARATION FOR THE MOVE

According to experienced structural movers, initial site preparations, excavation, tunneling, and jack setup for the average residential structure can take from one to two weeks. This time can be increased dramatically if site conditions are not favorable. Delays can be caused by the presence of sand or clay soils, large trees preventing or limiting access by equipment, high groundwater or tide schedule, or the presence of rock.

At this point in the process, the decision whether to move the house intact or partially or fully disassembled is implemented. Houses that are square or rectangular in shape are less complex to lift and move; therefore, garages, porches, wings, additions, or other attached structures on separate foundations are usually detached and moved independently. In a historic house move, portions that are not original or relevant to the history of the house are often cut away and discarded. If it is determined that the house will be moved intact with only minor cutting, the next step is to cut away those portions of the house and prepare the structure for excavation and shoring.

PREPARATIONS FOR LIFTING

A professional structural mover most likely has a rough idea of how the house will be supported when submitting his original estimate to the home owner. After a contract is signed, additional visits to both the existing and the new sites are made. After determining how loads are distributed through the house frame into the foundation and whether the house will be refurbished on the inside (cracking of the walls is acceptable since they will be redone) and on the basis of past experience, the structural mover will select a method that is the most efficient and economical for this move. A detailed plan indicating how the structure will be supported for the lifting, moving, and setting-down phases is submitted to the DOT. This plan is also outlined by the mover in drawing form and certified by a professional engineer. In many cities and towns, the additional drawings are required for the appropriation of a moving permit.

The plan will consist of a grid of support beams that will act as the temporary foundation while the house is relocated. These support beams are specifically placed to account for concentrated loads, such as chimneys and main load-bearing elements. Other requirements for placement may include obstructions or interferences along the travel route, such as trees, shrubs, tight turns, and utilities. It is also important to consider beam placements in relation to the new foundation.

Whether the house rests on a slab-on-grade or a wall-type foundation, excavation around the foundation is necessary in order to facilitate insertion of the support beams. Once the foundation is exposed, preparations for support beam placement to aid in lifting the structure can begin.

BEAM AND CRIBBING PLACEMENT

After exposing the foundation, the next step depends on the size and makeup of the house and its proximity to adjacent structures or obstructions. Houses come in all shapes and sizes, so movers have a variety of ways to lift and support them. To effectively explain the moving process, we will use an average-size timber-frame home with a fieldstone-wall foundation.

First, portions of the foundation walls are removed, allowing machinery and workers to easily access the basement, while other sections are punctured or cut at precise locations using a cable saw or a jackhammer for the insertion of lifting beams. Cribbing is then erected alongside the foundation and in the basement of the house. The cribbing is stacked in an alternating pattern to an elevation where the beams that will be threaded through the foundation can be temporarily set. The cribbing will also support the hydraulic jacks that will be used in lifting the house.

Next, a series of beams known as needle beams are inserted through the openings in the foundation, perpendicular to the length of the house. These beams are typically spaced between four and twelve feet apart, contingent on load, the location of supporting posts and girders, and the soundness of sills, and are placed below the sills atop the stacks of cribbing.

The cribbing offers a stable base that is essential in providing lateral resistance to the given loads. Once the house is lifted completely off its foundation, there is no longer any lateral or side-to-side support provided by the foundation walls. It is like supporting a shoe box on four pencils. If a load were applied to the shoe box perpendicular to the pencils, all the pencils would sway to one side, and the box would fall over. Now consider using four wooden blocks for support. The base of these blocks is wide and stable; thus, when a load is applied, it is transferred to the ground, similar to a foundation.

Cribbing is desirable when lifting loads by jacking stages. In this procedure, the cribbing will act as a platform for a hydraulic jack. After the needle beams are positioned under the house, the jacks are positioned below the ends of the needle beams and are ready for the first lift.

As the foundation work progresses, other members of the mover's team are bracing and shoring parts of the house that may pose a threat of collapse during the move. Typically, tall chimneys, porches, and structural members that relied on the old foundation for support are braced.

LIFT AND ROLL

The next step is to insert two or more large main load-bearing I beams or mains, parallel to the length of the house, below the needle beams on stacked cribbing. To perform this step, there needs to be sufficient room below the needle beams to accommodate the mains underneath. Depending on the site conditions, this can be achieved in a number of ways. Excavating down below the level of the needle beams, allowing the mains to fit underneath, would be ideal, but it isn't always possible.

In some instances, a site may have several constraints that may cause great difficulty in positioning the lifting beams. Trees or adjacent structures may require that the beams be placed after several rounds of lifting and excavating.

Once enough clearance exists below the needle beams, the mains are inserted and supported on the stacked cribbing. Next, jacks are placed on blocking at selected locations below the mains.

The mains will now receive the force of the jacks below them and the weight of the needle beams that support the house from above. These mains will also act as the frame under which rollers will be used to move the house off its existing foundation and also the mechanism under which dollies will be inserted and bolted to for the move.

The size and placement of these mains is based on the weight of the house, the weight of the steel needle beams, and all other bracing required for the move. In addition, these beams must also be positioned to account for obstructions encountered along the travel route and the new foundation. If the new foundation is to be completed prior to the arrival of the house, precise locations of block-outs in the new foundation to insert the temporary main and needle beams must be in place.

With the needle beams, temporary bracing, and shoring in place, the moment has come that will test the mover's skill and experience and the home owner's nerves. Jacks are independently pressurized, eliminating the effects of uneven cribbing and localized settlement. Next, the UJM is engaged, and several of the jacks extend upward, lifting the house as high as the jacks will go.

Next, additional cribbing is shimmed below the mains, where the jacks not used in the initial lift are located. The UJM is again engaged, and the jacks not used in the first lift extend upward as high as they can go. This technique may be repeated several times to attain the required height.

Next, roll beams are threaded below and perpendicular to the mains. These roll beams are also supported on cribbing and will be used similar in concept to railroad tracks. Rollers are placed beneath the mains and on the roll beams. The house is then lowered until it comes in contact with the rollers. In some cases, movers will simply use a series of rounded lead pipes instead of rollers, setting the mains directly on them.

After the roll beams are positioned correctly, the next step is to connect to the mains and to pull or push the main beam framing system laterally across the roll beams to the required location. In some cases, if the house is to be moved over a relatively short distance, the move can be achieved solely through the use of roll beams. However, if the move requires traveling over public streets, the next step will require the insertion of moving dollies.

THE MOVE

With the house off its foundation, the next step entails jacking and cribbing the structure high enough to wheel in a series of moving dollies that are, in essence, compact truck axles. These dollies are set below the mains, connected to each other, and bolted to the bottom flange of the mains. At this point, the truck, which will pull the house support system, is backed into position and attached. With the utility companies and police in position, the house is ready for its journey.

MOVING PARTIALLY OR TOTALLY DISASSEMBLED

If the house's size or shape prevents moving it in one piece, then cutting it into manageable pieces is the answer. The house may be too tall or wide for vertical and horizontal clearances along the travel route, such as underpasses, utility lines, or mature trees that cannot be cut. In many cases, chimneys and the roof of a house are partially or completely removed.

In frame construction, cuts in walls are made between studs using chainsaws for quick and rough cuts and reciprocating saws when clean cutting is required around window casings and doorjambs. Vertical cuts through roofs are usually made between or immediately adjacent to rafters or joists. In concrete block or CMU construction, sections of block may be removed and replaced at the new site. Cuts through concrete are typically made using jackhammers, diamond-impregnated cutting blades, or torches.

The technical aspects and equipment used in a partial move are very similar to a whole house move. If we use as an example a two-story house, once the second-floor sections are cut away from the first floor, the needle beams are threaded below the second-floor joists, and then a crane is used to lift the top portion of the house away. The bottom portion can also be moved the same way, or mains and roll beams can be utilized. In a partially dismantled move, interior bracing is increased dramatically. The forces in the frame of the house can no longer travel through the main load-carrying members since the house is cut up. The solution is the addition of interior bracing to aid in transferring the loads through the structure.

If the house is to be sliced into smaller pieces or totally disassembled, the mover will remove all windows, doors, cabinets, and fixtures—that is, all interior components. Next, the roof comes off; then the walls, including all framing elements and siding; and finally the floor and associated framing. As each piece is removed, it is documented and packaged on a reconstruction plan.

Reassembling a house will sometimes pose a challenge. Most houses settle over time, allowing framing to become out of plumb and the house to fall out of square, that is, when exterior walls converge at a corner and do not form ninety-degree angles. Once the house is ready to be reassembled, squaring and leveling equipment will be replaced by eyeballing. This will ensure that doors, windows, fixtures, and framing will fit properly.

THE VACATED SITE

The vacated site is subject to several requirements either from the new owners of that site or by state law. State laws vary on how the site must be left, but most agree on the following conditions:

1. *Sewer and water.* The sewer and water service lines must be properly capped at the service shutoff. Concrete can normally be used as a sewer cap.
2. *Foundation removal.* The foundation must be removed a minimum of twenty-four inches below grade.
3. *Basement slab.* The basement floor must be broken up to allow for proper drainage of the site.
4. *Debris removal.* Any construction debris is to be removed, not backfilled into the excavation.
5. *Backfill.* The excavation is to be backfilled with native material and seeded with grass seed if applicable.

In some cases, a house is moved to avoid demolition in making way for a new house. The owners of that site may have other requirements as to how the site is to be vacated. For example, they may not want the site filled in. It is important to have these issues documented so as not to be surprised after the house has been moved.

THE NEW FOUNDATION

Prior to the arrival of the house on-site, the structural mover has made a determination on when the foundation is to be constructed. The decision is based on the age and condition of the house as well as the project schedule.

With houses less than fifty years old, the foundation can be constructed prior to the arrival of the house onto the site. If the house is older than fifty years, the chances of its being out of square are increased. This makes the construction of the new foundation more difficult.

With a square foundation, if one measures the lengths of two sides, the other two sides will be the same, thus forming ninety-degree angles. With a foundation that is out of square, the sides are not equal, so extensive measurements must be taken to ensure a proper fit with the structure.

Foundations settle over time; the older the foundation, the greater the potential for settlement. With an old New England fieldstone foundation, settlement may have occurred over many years, shifting the house out of plumb; that is, vertical framing members do not form ninety-degree angles with floors or ceilings. Vertical elements that rest on the foundation will move along with it. Other framing elements that are connected to these main load-carrying vertical members will also shift to accommodate the settlement. This takes many years to occur, thus minimizing the amount of stress imparted to the framing elements.

When the timber-frame house is positioned on a square and level foundation, the members are forced back to their original locations instantaneously. This may cause racking or shifting of the frame, imparting stresses in members that were not designed for such forces and causing cracking in walls and/or ceilings where the stress is relieved. With masonry construction, the stresses translate into excessive cracking in the walls, particularly at the mortared joints.

To facilitate the appropriate placement of a house that is not square onto a new foundation, the contractor will first position the house over the location of the new foundation. With the house hovering overhead, accurate measurements of the structure in relation to the new foundation can be taken. Any imperfections due to the construction irregularities or caused by settlement can be measured and duplicated on the new foundation to virtually eliminate cracking. Finally, the new foundation is constructed up to meet the underside of the interior and exterior walls of the structure. This procedure is required with masonry structures or when a timber structure is to be preserved to highlight its original age characteristics.

One of the drawbacks in having a house hovering three feet over the proposed foundation is constructability. Since no machinery can squeeze under the house, the contractor is forced to hand dig to excavate for the construction of the foundation. This can become quite costly and extend the time of the project considerably. The question one should ask is, How sensitive is the interior of the house? With a historic house, cracking of the interior walls and ceilings could cause irreparable damage to architectural features, including woodwork and wallpaper. If the structure is not historic or if the interior will be reworked, time spent in precise measurements can be avoided.

Another important aspect of a new foundation is waterproofing. Protecting a basement from water infiltration is vital to the survival of the structure. When wood is subjected to moist air or water over a long period of time, the result is rot and mold, both of which decrease the strength of structural members.

There are many ways water can enter a basement: through the walls of a foundation, from below the base slab, or even as water vapor coming in through an open window. To account for this, several different types of waterproofing can be used, depending on material, application, and budget. In the absence of a water table, damp-proofing should be applied at a minimum. Damp-proofing is necessary for below-grade habitable building spaces.

Figure 7.4 shows a carpenter making final adjustments to the sill plates prior to setting the house on its new foundation. Notice the dark sprayed-on waterproofing membrane applied to the outside walls of the foundation. Sometimes insulating sheathing is added over the waterproofing membrane, as shown, to provide additional insulation for exte-

FIGURE 7.4
A house positioned on its new foundation.
Courtesy of Hayden Building Movers, Cotuit, Massachusetts.

rior sidings, such as brick or wood, hardboard, aluminum, and vinyl sidings.

Openings in the walls of the foundation will accommodate the roll and needle beams as the house is reverse-jacked into position on its new foundation. Once the house is in place, all the support beams would be removed and the openings filled in or left as windows.

SETTING THE HOUSE IN PLACE

Prior to the arrival of the house onto the new site, clearing, excavation, and grading are necessary to allow construction to begin and to ensure that the house can be maneuvered onto the site. When the new foundation is constructed prior to the arrival of the house, portions of it are left out temporarily. This is done to accommodate the needle beams that will support the house while it is being lowered into place. The process works in the reverse manner from when the house was raised off its original foundation.

First, cribbing is set below the main beams with jacks positioned on them to execute the first lift. This lift will allow the travel dollies to be removed and roll beams with rollers to be inserted below the mains. Next, the house is rolled over the new foundation, then cribbed and jacked until the house rests on its new foundation with the needle beams protruding out from the temporary openings in the foundation. Finally, the needle beams are removed and the holes in the foundation filled. The remaining tasks include reestablishing all the utility connections, site grading, and landscaping.

MOVING A HOUSE BY BARGE

A barge is a flat-bottomed vessel that works on inland waterways and is one of this country's earliest modes of transporting goods and people. The inland waterway system consists of rivers, canals, bays, sounds, and lakes as well as the intercoastal waterways. There are about 25,000 miles of navigable waterways in the contiguous United States.

Most barges do not operate under their own power but rather require the use of tugboats to propel them. Barges vary in size and typically carry coal, oil, petroleum chemicals, wood, cement, asphalt, ore, garbage, and sometimes structures.

As with any house move, moving by barge comes with a variety of requirements and constraints. The following list outlines the most common aspects to consider before employing the use of a barge:

Obstructions
- *Bridges.* Although utilities are avoided, as with a road move, the clearance below a bridge can stop a move in its wake. However, on many rivers and canals with major water traffic, the bridges can be raised and lowered to accommodate a variety of water vessels.
- *Ship traffic.* There are approximately 6,000 tugs and 30,000 barges at work in the United States, not to mention a variety of other vessels utilizing the waterways. The chances of facing a traffic problem can be relatively high, especially in rivers and canals.
- *Environmental issues.* There are many environmental issues and permitting requirements when moving by barge. From endangered sea grasses and mangroves to tropical trees and shrubbery to nesting animals such as terns and turtles, environmental concerns play a major role in barge travel.

Weather and Timing

- *Tides.* The periodic rise and fall of the ocean water levels that occurs every twelve hours, produced by the attraction of the sun and moon, dictate when a barge can be safely loaded or unloaded to avoid getting stuck or grounded on the sea bottom. This phenomenon does not affect rivers and lakes unless they are located close to and feed into an ocean.
- *Schedule.* The barge is typically reserved several months in advance unless the structural mover owns one. It may take some time merely to schedule the barge, depending on how busy the barge is and the day or night of the week that is chosen for the move. Then weather may or may not cooperate. In some instances, weather can interfere with a move, holding up the barge and affecting your moving schedule as well as the mover's and barge owner's schedules.

Cost Factors

- *Size.* The size and weight of the structure being moved and the depth of waterway when traveling, loading, and unloading will factor into the size and draft (the depth of the barge below water) of the barge selected for a move.
- *Type.* Although some barges are self-propelled, most are pushed or pulled by tugboats. It is safer to use two tugboats in case one breaks down, especially if there is a current in the water. Depending on the load and size of the barge, one tugboat could manage if it had to, but two are optimal.
- *Loading and unloading.* Barges often run aground or become stuck on sandbars and beaches in the loading and unloading phases of a move. This can be very expensive in two ways: schedule and damages.

Usually, if a barge becomes stuck, the move is postponed for twelve hours until the next high tide. This translates into scheduling conflicts and may mean that additional equipment will be required to help free the barge from the obstruction. These costs may be billed to you unless stated otherwise in the contract.

Damages may occur in the area where the barge became stuck, specifically, property, animal life, or environmental damages. Damages could cost more than the move itself.

To avoid these damages, barges of different drafts are sometimes used on the same job. One barge is pushed or pulled in the deep water, and the other is used when the load is to be brought into shallow water.

- *Duration.* The amount of time that the barge needs to be used—including the time it takes to arrive on-site to transport the house, travel time to the new site, the time it takes to offload, and the time it will take for the barge to return to its original location—must all be included in the cost of the barge.

- *Navigation charges.* Most inland navigation authorities charge for a barge to use their waters. The mover will pay these charges, but, of course, in the end the home owner will pay for this charge.

- *Mooring fees.* If you are required to moor or dock the barge in a port because of poor weather or delays in the move, the fees can add up quickly. The costs of securing the barge, securing the house so that it does not fall into the water, and delaying the barge's departure to its next scheduled project are all charged to the mover and then passed along to the home owner.

- *Additional material and equipment.* It is common for additional fill material to be brought to the loading and unloading site to compensate for the difference in elevation between the deck of the barge and land. Usually, when additional sand is necessary, environmental requirements state that the sand be of native origin to the site. Getting the material and the equipment to put it in place can be costly and time consuming to the mover. Of course, you know who ultimately covers the costs.

In the end, the structural mover will try to strike a balance between cost, type, capacity, and schedule that will best fit the specific project.

USING A CRANE

A crane can move a house partially or totally disassembled with relative ease and efficiency (see chapter 8), but using one can be very expensive. Rental fees range between $120 and $130 per hour for a small 15-ton model up to $500 per hour for the 1,000-ton models.

Cranes are designed for both general use and specific purposes. Each type, model, or size of crane manufactured may have different operating controls and require specialized operator training, individualized inspection criteria, and different preventive maintenance schedules.

8

The Economics of House Moving

As with most projects, the question remains the same: How much will it cost? With a house move, this question can have a variety of answers, depending on many variables. In this chapter, we identify and discuss the most common variables, present a system for determining the costs associated with a house move, and provide several examples that demonstrate the procedure in calculating a "ballpark" figure of your house-moving project.

FACTORS IN DETERMINING COSTS

The structural mover determines the cost in moving a house by considering the amount and type of equipment needed for the move and the duration of the move. The majority of work is in the preparations for the move; therefore, most of the cost is calculated on that basis. The distance a house must travel becomes relative to the cost when site conditions are difficult. The following factors will dictate the cost of moving a house:

Makeup of the house. The type of material used in the construction of the house will dictate the weight of the structure and the size of the members required to lift and move it. As previously discussed, a timber-frame house is much lighter than a masonry or brick house, which requires much larger members to support it.

Size and shape of the house. The size of the house will enable the mover to quantify the amount of equipment needed to lift and support the structure. A rectangular or square house is much easier to move than an L- or a T-shaped house. With an L or a T shape, the house may need to be cut to fit across a roadway. A two-story house may require cutting to avoid utility lines.

Foundation. The type of foundation and accessibility to it will influence the cost greatly. The amount of clearance under the structure will affect the type of excavation equipment needed to dig out portions of the foundation for insertion of beams. If access is minimal (less than three feet), hand digging may be required, thus increasing the labor cost substantially. The duration of the moving process is increased and may require the structural mover to forgo other jobs because of a lack of manpower or equipment. The company may charge more to compensate for lost business opportunities.

Site accessibilities. Gaining access to and from both sites will influence the types and sizes of equipment needed for the move.

Travel route. The route the house must traverse to the new site will dictate the amount of permitting required (see chapter 3), the size of the equipment the mover can use, and accessibility issues. Such accessibility issues include low bridges or those not designed to handle the weight of a house and associated equipment, terrain and types of roads, historic trees that preclude their being cut, and town centers through which the house may not be allowed to travel, all of which can increase the travel route and expenses.

Utilities. The cost of temporarily removing utility lines varies from state to state. Massachusetts is the only state that holds the utility companies responsible for costs associated with the temporary removal and resetting of utility lines. The costs associated with wire removal and resetting can be quite substantial in some states (see tables 8.2, 8.3, and 8.4).

Temporary living expenses. The typical move takes from one to two days, and reconnecting utilities may take weeks. Some thought should be given to finding an alternate place to stay while the house is being put back together.

CALCULATING COSTS

The following tables can be used to calculate a "ballpark" figure for your moving project. The information provided was gathered from interviews with building movers, utility company representatives, magazines, news-

Table 8.1. House-Moving Expenses

Structure and Construction Type	Lift Only	Lot Move	Move on Roads			Old Foundation Basement Height		New Concrete Foundation
			Intact	Partial	Total	>5 feet	<5 feet	
Timber frame								
Cape (24 × 36 feet) or ranch								
Less than 50 years old	$ 8,000	$ 10,000	$ 20,000	$ 25,000	$ 35,000	$0	$ 5,000	$12,000
Between 50 and 100 years old	$12,000	$ 15,000	$ 30,000	$ 35,000	$ 55,000	$0	$ 5,000	$12,000
Over 100 years old	$16,000	$ 20,000	$ 40,000	$ 45,000	$ 75,000	$0	$ 5,000	$12,000
Colonial style (38 × 46 feet)								
Less than 50 years old	$12,000	$ 15,000	$ 30,000	$ 35,000	$ 55,000	$0	$10,000	$18,000
Between 50 and 100 years old	$16,000	$ 20,000	$ 40,000	$ 45,000	$ 75,000	$0	$10,000	$18,000
Over 100 years old	$20,000	$ 30,000	$ 50,000	$ 60,000	$ 95,000	$0	$10,000	$18,000
Large house (40 × 120 feet, three story)	$50,000	$100,000	$120,000	$160,000	$200,000	$0	$20,000	$30,000
Barn (40 × 80 feet)	$20,000	$ 40,000	$150,000	$180,000	$210,000	$0	$ 3,000	$16,000
Garage (two car)	$10,000	$ 15,000	$ 20,000	$ 25,000	$ 35,000	$0	$ 2,000	$ 8,000
Masonry								
Ranch or bungalow (20 × 40 feet)								
With slab attached								
Less than 75 years old	$30,000	$ 60,000	$120,000	n/a	n/a	n/a	n/a	n/a
Over 100 years old	$60,000	$120,000	$240,000	n/a	n/a	n/a	n/a	n/a

Notes: New concrete foundation is assumed to be full basement height except for barn and garage foundations.
Moving by barge will cost at a minimum $10,000; this includes a day for the barge to travel to the site, a day for the move with one tugboat, and a day for the barge to return home. Anything more is extra.
Renting a crane can range between $120 per hour for a 15-ton crane to $275 per hour for a 100-ton crane. Rental includes the equipment and operator, typically with a four-hour minimum. Charges begin at the rental yard.
For historic house moving, a factor of 1.5 should be applied to figures except utilities. This factor accounts for the fragile state of the structure and the accuracy with which the new foundation is to be constructed.
For barns older than 50 years, a factor of 1.3 should be applied.
For badly deteriorated masonry structures, a factor of 1.2 should be applied.
For moving or removing a tree, add $600.
For disposal of concrete waste, add $65 per ton (one ton = 2,000 pounds).
Landscaping is not included in any of the figures provided.
$0 = no cost.

Table 8.2. Utility Wire Fees

The following fees represent the cost associated with lifting and temporarily detaching and reattaching wires

Electric	$3,500 per crew per day, two-crew minimum; dependent on number of wires and length of move
Phone	$1,000 per crew per day, two-crew minimum
Cable	$1,000 per crew per day, two-crew minimum

Table 8.3. Police Detail

Police may be required for traffic control	
Dependent on complexity of traffic situation	
Four junior officers	$2,500 per day

Table 8.4. New Site Expenses

Water	$6,000 for new connection, includes a maximum length of 50 feet of pipe from the main; $16 per foot thereafter
Sewer	$8,000 for new connection, includes a maximum length of 50 feet of pipe from the main; $18 per foot thereafter
Septic	$10,000 to $14,000, depending on the size of the system
Electric	Minor expense with a maximum wire length of 150 feet; beyond requires new poles at $500 per pole and $13 per foot of line
Phone	Minor expense with a maximum wire length of 180 feet; same as electrical, and $11 per foot
Gas	Free connection up to 75 feet from existing main; $12 per foot thereafter; if no main, then not feasible
Landscape	Dependent on owner preferences
Reconnection of utilities vary from state to state, some are minor; budget $4,000	

paper articles, and personal experience. The figures represent an estimate of costs associated with a straightforward move lacking complexity and unforeseen difficulties. Costs vary from state to state; for an accurate assessment of cost related to your project, contact a structural mover.

Several sample moves are provided here to help you use these tables.

EXAMPLE 1

The house is a nonhistoric timber-frame, Cape Cod–style home approximately forty-five years old with a basement height of six feet. The move can be performed with the house remaining intact. The house is to travel five miles, avoiding the center of town through a residential area with approximately ten utility lines requiring removal or lifting.

The new site is easy to access. Utilities include electric, phone, cable, and water connections forty-five feet from the closest face of the house. A gas and sewer main does not exist. It is anticipated that the move will take one day.

Estimate

Since the house is nonhistoric and does not require "special" attention, choose "Cape," "Less than 50 years old," "Move on Roads," "Intact" ($20,000). Next, since the basement height is greater than five feet, there is no additional cost for extensive excavation ($0). The new concrete foundation is $10,000.

Since only ten utility lines require attention and the move is estimated at one day, electric will be $3,500 × two crews; phone, $1,000 × two crews; and cable, $1,000 × two crews. The cost in Massachusetts for this portion of the move is $0. There will be a police detail required all day at a cost of $2,500.

At the new site, since all the major utilities are forty-five feet from the house, costs will be as follows: water, $6,000; electric, $100; phone, $100; and reconnections, $4,000. Gas is unavailable since a main does not exist, and since there is no city sewer, a septic system may cost $14,000.

EXAMPLE 2

The house is a historic timber-frame, Cape Cod–style home approximately 175 years old with a basement height of six feet. The move can be performed with the house being partially disassembled. The house is to travel fifteen miles through the center of town through a relatively congested area with approximately seventy-five utility lines requiring removal or lifting.

The new site is difficult to access with utilities including electric, phone, cable, and water connections 375 feet from the closest face of the house.

Table 8.5. Estimated Project Cost: Example 1

		Alternate Solution: Partially disassembling the house to avoid utilities, then using a crane.	
Mover	$20,000	Partial disassembly	$25,000
Foundation contractor	$10,000	Foundation contractor	$10,000
Utility relocation costs		Crane:One full day	
Electric	$ 7,000	15-ton crane	
Phone	$ 2,000	(one 12-hour day)	
Cable	$ 2,000	($120/hours × 12 hours)	$ 1,400
Police detail	$ 2,500	Police detail	$ 2,500
New site costs		New site costs	
Water	$ 6,000	Water	$ 6,000
Electric	$ 100	Electric	$ 100
Phone	$ 100	Phone	$ 100
Reconnect	$ 4,000	Reconnect	$ 4,000
Sewer	$14,000	Sewer	$14,000
Total	$67,700	Total	$63,100

A gas and sewer main does not exist. It is anticipated the move itself will take three days.

Estimate

Since the house is historic and requires "special" considerations, a factor of 1.5 will be assessed for each cost; choose "Cape," "Over 100 years old," "Move on Roads," "Partial" ($45,000 × 1.5). Next, since the basement height is greater than five feet, there is no additional cost for extensive excavation ($0). The new concrete foundation is $10,000 × 1.5.

Since seventy-five utility lines require attention and the move is estimated at three days, electric will be $3,500 × three days × three crews; phone, $1,000 × three days × three crews; and cable, $1,000 × three days × three crews. The cost in Massachusetts for this portion of the move is $0. There will be a police detail required all day at a cost of $2,500 × three days × two details.

Since all major utilities are 375 feet from the house at the new site, costs will be as follows: water, $6,000 + 375 feet − 50 feet = 325 feet at $16 per foot = $5,200; electric, $100 + 375 feet − 150 feet = 225 feet, so one pole at $500 + 225 feet × 13 feet of new line = $2,995; phone, $100 + 375 feet − 150 feet = 225 feet, and use of electric pole + 225 feet × $11 per foot of new line = $2,475; ($0); and reconnections ($4,000). Gas is unavailable since a main does not exist, and since there is no city sewer, a septic system may cost $14,000.

EXAMPLE 3

The barn is a timber frame structure thirty by sixty feet with no basement and is approximately seventy-five years old. The move can be performed with the barn intact. The barn is to travel 150 feet back from the road. There are no utility lines except electrical service to the barn.

Estimate

The barn is seventy-five years old and nonhistoric and does not require "special" attention; choose "Barn," "Greater than 50 years old" (and multiply by a factor of 1.3), "Lot Move," "Intact ($40,000 × 1.3). Next, since there is no basement, addition costs are $3,000 × 1.3. The new concrete foundation is $16,000 × 1.3.

Since this is a lot move, utility fees are minimal.

EXAMPLE 4

The house is a large Colonial-style historic timber frame measuring thirty-eight by forty-six feet with a three-foot crawl space and is approximately 250 years old. The move must be performed with the house intact because of its interior architectural significance. The house must travel a total of five miles, avoiding the center of town because of extensive obstacles and

Table 8.6. Estimated Project Cost: Example 2

Mover	$ 67,500
Foundation contractor	$ 15,000
Utility relocation costs	
Electric	$ 31,500
Phone	$ 9,000
Cable	$ 9,000
Police detail	$ 15,000
New site costs	
Water	$ 11,200
Electric	$ 3,525
Phone	$ 2,575
Reconnect	$ 4,000
Sewer	$ 14,000
Total	$182,300

Table 8.7. Estimated Project Cost: Example 3

Mover	$52,000
Foundation contractor	$24,700
Utility relocation costs	$0
New site costs	
Electric	$ 100
Total	$76,800

utilities. To accomplish this, the house will travel by barge two miles downriver to its new site.

The new site is located less than a mile from the river and can easily access utility reconnections. It is anticipated that the move will take two days.

Estimate

Since the house is historic and requires "special" considerations, a factor of 1.5 will be assessed for each cost; choose "Colonial style," "Over 100 years old," "Move on Roads," "Intact" ($50,000 × 1.5). Next, since the basement height is less than five feet, there is an additional cost for extensive excavation ($10,000). The new concrete foundation is $18,000 × 1.5.

The cost for the barge is estimated at $10,000 × 1.5. Since most of the utility lines will be avoided, the costs should be as follows: electric, $3,500

Table 8.8. Estimated Project Cost: Example 4

Mover	$ 85,000
Foundation contractor	$ 27,000
Barge (mover)	$ 15,000
Utility relocation costs	
Electric	$ 14,000
Phone	$ 4,000
Cable	$ 4,000
Police detail	$ 10,000
New site costs	
Water	$ 6,000
Electric	$ 100
Phone	$ 100
Reconnect	$ 4,000
Sewer	$ 8,000
Total	$177,200

× two days × two crews; phone, $1,000 × two days × two crews; and cable, $1,000 × two days × two crews. The cost in Massachusetts for this portion of the move is $0. There will be a police detail required all day at a cost of $2,500 × two days × two details).

At the new site, since all the major utilities are readily available and in short proximity, the budget is $4,000. Costs will be as follows: water, $6,000; sewer, $8,000; electric, $100; phone, $100; and reconnections, $4,000.

9

A Case Study: Strawbery Banke

Strawbery Banke opened to the public in 1965 and continues to promote and preserve Portsmouth's heritage and to attract visitors and has become a major asset to the local economy.

Located two miles from the mouth of the Piscataqua River in Portsmouth, New Hampshire, Strawbery Banke exists as a historic waterfront neighborhood museum consisting of over forty structures on ten acres of land. The site was originally named for the thick growth of wild berries along the west bank of the Piscataqua River by a group of English settlers under the leadership of Captain Walter Neal in 1630. The settlers' primary objective was to establish a colony for economic reasons on behalf of a group of London merchants who called themselves the Laconia Company.

Former governor of Newfoundland, Captain John Mason, who had received a large grant of land in America, ran the Laconia Company from England. Robert Carse writes in his book *Ports of Call* about Captain John Mason and his Laconia Company:

> Their purpose was to take an almost immediate profit from both the fur trade and the offshore fisheries. Mason, who had served for six years as governor of Newfoundland, knew about the money to be made from fishing. He believed that a post established at the mouth of the Piscataqua could attract a good part of the Canadian traffic in pelts by way of Lake Champlain and the upper reaches of the river.

In 1638, after several years of exploration and failed attempts at establishing trade, the Laconia Company went bankrupt. The Strawbery Banke settlement declared allegiance to the King of England, but lacking in their ability to enforce local disputes and laws, the Massachusetts Bay Colony, in 1641, extended its jurisdiction over them.

In 1653, after petitioning the Massachusetts General Court, Strawbery Banke was renamed Portsmouth. In the 1700s, as Portsmouth matured and expanded, an elite group of merchants and their families dominated Portsmouth's trade and politics. The Wentworths, who had firsthand knowledge of English society and sophistication, would become one of New Hampshire's most powerful colonial families.

Portsmouth's strong trade continued through the 1760s but was interrupted by the American Revolution. In 1800, Portsmouth once again was well on its way in becoming one of the leading ports of trade in America until the depletion of timber in and around the Piscataqua region forced the town to shift to shipbuilding and manufacturing.

In the nineteenth century, the area once dominated by sea captains and artisans would slowly come to be occupied by European immigrants. By 1907, the area know as Puddle Dock was backfilled, leaving little evidence of a once lively maritime center.

FIGURE 9.1
A view of Strawbery Banke today, across what was once Puddle Dock. The dark building is the Jones House, built circa 1790.
Courtesy of the author.

FIGURE 9.2
The Puddle Dock area at Strawbery Banke.
Courtesy of the Collection of Strawbery Banke Museum, Portsmouth, New Hampshire.

With a lack of upkeep and the decay of wharves, the area began to be filled in. During the 1930s, two members of the Portsmouth Historical Society, John Mead Howells and Stephen Decatur, proposed the creation of a historic area made up of old houses in the city's south end, including the old Puddle Dock neighborhood. However, the world's attention focused on World War II, and the proposal was tabled indefinitely.

In the 1950s, a federal urban renewal project threatened the Puddle Dock neighborhood. Prompted by the city's librarian, Dorothy M. Vaughan, concerned citizens and preservationists formed a committee to save Portsmouth's heritage. Taking its name from the first settlement at the mouth of the Piscataqua River, Strawbery Banke, Inc., was organized in 1958 as a nonprofit educational organization to prevent the planned demolition of the Puddle Dock neighborhood. After amending the New Hampshire law permitting restoration as a part of renewal, the Portsmouth Housing Authority acquired the land and buildings, arranged for the relocation of residents, and had several nineteenth- and twentieth-century buildings removed. All other buildings along with ten acres of land were deeded to Strawbery Banke, Inc. In doing so, the site was the first in the country where a federal urban renewal parcel was turned over to an educational institution for the purpose of preservation.

THE JOSHUA WENTWORTH HOUSE: HISTORIC AND ARCHITECTURAL SIGNIFICANCE

In 1770, a successful merchant and future dedicated patriot, Joshua Wentworth, purchased a small house on Hanover Street in Portsmouth in hopes of expanding it into a larger dwelling. The grandson of Lieutenant Governor John Wentworth, nephew of Governor Benning Wentworth, and cousin of New Hampshire's last royal governor, Joshua was one of the richest men in Portsmouth.

At the time, the Wentworths dominated trade, politics, and Portsmouth's social structure. Although Joshua Wentworth shared the same last name as some of the most influential people in Portsmouth, he was never part of the inner workings of the Wentworth family.

In 1776, Joshua Wentworth pledged his loyalty to the colonial cause for

FIGURE 9.3
The Joshua Wentworth House as it once stood on Hanover Street in the early part of the nineteenth century.
Courtesy of the Collection of Strawbery Banke Museum, Portsmouth, New Hampshire.

independence and as a continental agent of New Hampshire helped orga-
nize the Continental Congress. He was elected to the Continental Congress in 1779 but chose to stay in Portsmouth, where he served as a state
representative and senator.

The Wentworth House is an outstanding example of Portsmouth's
architecture in the late 1700s and typifies the family's knowledge and
appreciation of fine architecture. Three other Wentworth properties—the
Benning Wentworth, Wentworth–Gardneer, and Governor John Wentworth houses—contained similar interior architectural features. The cor-
nices, mantelpieces, and other interior refinements on the interior of Joshua's house indicate a difference in scale with respect to other architectural
features within the house. It is believed that the woodwork in the house
may actually have been fabricated for the much larger Governor John
Wentworth mansion, fifty miles northwest of Portsmouth, in Wolfeboro,
New Hampshire.

Governor John Wentworth had commissioned architect Peter Harrison
of Newport, Rhode Island, to design his house, making it one of the largest
mansions at the time. However, at the start of the American Revolution,
Royal Governor John Wentworth fled to England, never to be seen again.
It is believed that because of the considerable amount of time required to
fashion the elaborate woodwork for his house and his premature departure, leaving the woodwork in the craftsman's shop, Joshua Wentworth,
having an appreciation for fine architecture, saw it fit to have the pieces
set into his home.

The Joshua Wentworth House is considered one of the most significant
prerevolutionary interpretations of English Georgian architecture. Prior to
its expansion by Joshua Wentworth, the original house was a four-room
dwelling. The evidence suggests that the original part of the house exists
behind the two chimneys. The front portion of the house, about twenty
feet deep and forty-six feet long, was added along with a new roof over
the entire structure and a kitchen on the east side. The exterior of this
nine-room house is close to its appearance at the time when it was completed, prior to the American Revolution.

It has two chimneys, a central hall, and a gable roof with five of the six
original dormers. Although a few features have been destroyed or altered,
including the front door, the scroll pediments over the dormer windows,

a dormer on the rear of the house, and a kitchen wing, we are aware of their prior existence as they were recorded in the 1937 Historic American Building Survey (HABS).

The interior finish woodwork is contained in the four front rooms and stair hall. Each of these rooms contains a fireplace with ornate treatment. Of the four rooms, the two located on the east side of the house are more distinctive. On the first floor, the eastern room (figure 9.4) contains an elaborate mantelpiece with carved consoles, marble hearth and jambs, and an overmantel panel (figure 9.5). In addition, the room contains a full modillioned Ionic cornice and four corner pilasters with Ionic capitals, architraves, and friezes (figure 9.6). On the second floor, the eastern room contains another mantelshelf ornamented with carved acanthus buds and scallop shells and with marble jambs and hearth (figure 9.7). The cornice in this room is also of the Ionic order, but the four corner pilasters are without true capitals.

All these features could have been suggested from illustrations of a 1727 book by William Kent titled *The Designs of Inigo Jones*. The book was believed to have existed in the private library of architect Peter Harrison and well known in Portsmouth as a direct source for the design of Governor Benning Wentworth's exquisite mantelpiece. It is also believed that two books by Batty Langley, *The Builders Director* (1746) and *The Builders Jewel* (1746), both available in Portsmouth around 1768, may also have contributed to some of the woodwork designs.

The interior of the Joshua Wentworth House represents a unique regional interpretation of English Palladian architecture utilizing advanced design resources and local workmanship. The house was one of the eight buildings in the city of Portsmouth that was recorded in the 1937 HABS and was ultimately placed on the National Register of Historic Places on July 2, 1971.

ECONOMIC RESOURCES

The relocation and preservation efforts of the Joshua Wentworth House began in 1970, when the Winebaum News Service donated the vacated house to Strawbery Banke. The house, which was used as an office, and the adjoining brick building with an estimated market value of $50,000 were located in the Vaughan Street Federal Urban Renewal Area and were

FIGURE 9.4
The Joshua Wentworth House.
Courtesy of the Collection of Strawbery Banke Museum, Portsmouth, New Hampshire.

scheduled to be demolished. Original estimates from structural movers for moving the house, constructing the new foundation, and setting the house in place ranged from $60,000 to $70,000.

In all moves prior to the relocation of the Joshua Wentworth House, Strawbery Banke appropriated funding for acquiring, situating, moving, and restoring houses set for demolition primarily through public contributions. With the passing of the 1966 National Historic Preservation Act allowing for federal grants for historic preservation and Department of Housing and Urban Development (HUD) funding available for urban renewal efforts, resources that were once nonexistent were now within an application's reach (see chapter 4).

There were two requirements in receiving federal funding. First, the Joshua Wentworth House would have to be placed on the National Register of Historic Places, and, second, appropriated funding must be available. Confirming the house's historic value would be easy since it was one of the first recorded in New Hampshire after HABS began in the 1930s.

FIGURE 9.5
The Joshua Wentworth House.
Courtesy of the Collection of Strawbery Banke Museum, Portsmouth, New Hampshire.

FIGURE 9.6
The Joshua Wentworth House.
Courtesy of the Collection of Strawbery Banke Museum, Portsmouth, New Hampshire.

FIGURE 9.7
The Joshua Wentworth House.
Courtesy of the Collection of Strawbery Banke Museum, Portsmouth, New Hampshire.

The HABS archives in the Library of Congress contains twenty-five sheets of measured drawings of the house made in 1934 and thirteen photographs made in 1935 and 1937.

In addition to filing an application with the National Park Service, Strawbery Banke solicited the endorsement of several organizations through letters approbating Strawbery Banke's efforts in obtaining federal funding to save the house. Such letters were sent to the Portsmouth Housing Authority (PHA), the local agency in charge of appropriating federal funding from HUD. Organizations such as Colonial Williamsburg, HABS, the Society for the Preservation of New England Antiquities, and the Association for Preservation Technology of Syracuse University all sent letters overwhelmingly supporting the preservation efforts of the Joshua Wentworth House.

After the first of several delays in moving the house, the Wentworth House was placed on the National Register, and the PHA granted Strawbery Banke 75 percent of up to $50,000 available through HUD to facilitate the move. This translated to $12,500 that Strawbery Banke had to provide in addition to engineering fees, consultant fees, and any restoration costs above the foundation level. To finance these additional expenses, Strawbery Banke applied for a matching grant from the National Park Service.

With grants from the National Park Service and the PHA, participation from more than twenty-two preservation organizations, generous gifts from more than twenty-five states, and continued local support, the Joshua Wentworth House now sits at the southeast corner of the intersection of Hancock and Washington streets at Strawbery Banke.

PLANNING THE MOVE

Strawbery Banke, Inc., was accustomed to moving historic houses for preservation. Prior to the Joshua Wentworth House move, Strawbery Banke had moved four other houses threatened with demolition onto its parcel: the Daniel Webster House in 1961, the Goodwin Mansion in 1963, Stoodley's Tavern in 1966, and the Walsh House in 1969. Moving the Wentworth House would pose a different set of challenges.

Planning for the move of the Joshua Wentworth House began in 1970. At the time, it was thought that the Wentworth House would be moved as Stoodley's Tavern was, being cut and braced in the same fashion and traveling on practically the same route.

The house was located on 119 Hanover Street, and after some lengthy discussions on where it would be placed, a decision was made to relocate the house to the southeast corner of the intersection of Hancock and Washington streets at Strawbery Banke. It was believed that the house would be cut in half with a travel route along the northern edge of the Vaughn Street Federal Urban Renewal Area: west on Hanover Street a short distance to Vaughn Street, south on Vaughn Street to Congress Street, east on Congress Street, through Market Square and east on Daniel Street and through the Bridge Plaza to State Street, east to Marcy Street, south to Hancock, and west to the new site.

Letters of intent were then sent to local utilities and the Portsmouth Fire and Police Departments. The letters requested estimates of the costs associated with handling electric power, telephone, fire alarm, wires and traffic control signals along the route. The dimensions of the house were given as forty-six feet wide and thirty-eight feet six inches deep with twenty-nine feet from the sill to the roof ridge. The loaded height was estimated at thirty-four feet above the ground. At the same time, it was determined that the character-defining architectural features of the Wentworth House were too important and sensitive to be cut or otherwise disturbed. A new travel route was suggested, taking the house through the northern end of Portsmouth's urban renewal area. Razing of existing buildings designated for demolition within the renewal area was well under way, and most of the obstructions had been cleared.

At about the same time, Strawbery Banke would face its first major hurdle. The positioning of the Joshua Wentworth House on the new site would require a variance. The Wentworth House did not meet the property line setback requirements set forth by the City of Portsmouth zoning ordinances. The Wentworth House was too close to the building directly behind it. Strawbery Banke sent a letter to the Portsmouth Zoning Board of Appeals stating probable hardship from denial. The letter stressed the financial hardship to Strawbery Banke if the variance were to be denied, and an alternate parcel was to be chosen on the Strawbery Banke property. The following points were used to convey Strawbery Banke's position:

1. A more restricted route for transporting the house would be required, making it necessary to cut the house into parts to be reassembled later. Such a route would lengthen the moving process.

2. Moving the house in parts would jeopardize its architectural integrity. It would also require extensive bracing to support the house structurally.

3. Foundation costs would increase in part because of the selection of alternate sites containing clay deposits and a high water table.

4. Rejection of this site would alter Strawbery Banke's plan of positioning houses acquired from other parts of Portsmouth into one area. All the other houses located here—the Daniel Webster House, the Governor Goodwin Mansion, and Stoodley's Tavern—would complement the Joshua Wentworth House.

5. The parking situation would not meet the urban renewal requirements as to the allotted quantity.

6. Costs incurred by Strawbery Banke to date from soil borings, engineering services and plans for the construction of the foundation at the proposed site would be irretrievable.

This letter, along with a letter from the owner of the adjacent property stating no objection to the placement of the Joshua Wentworth House, convinced the Portsmouth Zoning Board to grant the variance to Strawbery Banke.

The next test for the project came when the City of Portsmouth required that the contractor remove the roof and the fireplaces within the building because of the narrowness of the streets and the difficulty of the topography. This was not good news for Strawbery Banke. The project was already suffering from a series of delays that threatened federal and local funding, and with this new challenge the possibility of its being canceled became more apparent. The removal of the roof and fireplaces was not an option for Strawbery Banke. Cutting off these elements would damage irreplaceable portions of the house.

In a conversation at a local pub, an idea surfaced that would became the saving grace for the project. It was decided that the Joshua Wentworth House would be loaded onto a barge and floated down the Piscataqua River to Strawbery Banke. The house would be moved in an easterly direction from its original site on Hanover Street to Vaughn Street, where it would make its way to the pier and be loaded onto a barge. Once secured, it would be floated down the Piscataqua River, under the Memorial Bridge, coming ashore near the Strawbery Banke parking lot adjacent to

Hancock Street. It would then travel a short distance across Marcy Street through the parking lot to its new site next to Stoodley's Tavern.

An additional extension was requested by the structural mover in order to acquire the necessary insurance to allow for the total coverage of the house during the move from land onto the barge and back to land again and also for the opportunity to take advantage of fairer weather and high tides. The difficulty came in insuring the house for the time during which it was being loaded and unloaded from the barge. At this critical point of transfer, it is difficult to hold a single party liable for any damage claims or destruction of the house.

It was determined that insurance could not be obtained during the period when the house was moved from land to the barge and from the barge back to land. For the project to proceed, Strawbery Banke had to assume full responsibility for the transitioning land-to-barge-to-land portions of the move. An agreement was struck and a contract signed that further stated that in the event of a total or partial destruction of the house, rendering it impossible to relocate the structure onto its new foundation, the structural mover would be entitled to recover all costs associated with removal of the debris. It also stated that in the event the house was damaged but still movable, the structural mover was entitled to receive full payment minus damages to the house.

PREPARATION FOR THE MOVE

While removing portions of the masonry chimney to prepare the house for the move, the structural mover identified deficiencies in the masonry that would threaten the stability of the chimneys during the move. Strawbery Banke hired a structural engineering consultant to inspect the foundations of both chimneys. The consultant's findings concurred with those of the structural mover in that both chimneys appeared structurally sound above the first floor but that both exhibited very weak masonry foundations below that point.

The structural engineering consultant believed that supporting members were framed into the chimneys. The structural mover disagreed, citing that there was no evidence of this and that, based on the mover's experience with other historical buildings in the Portsmouth area, the shoring of all floors in the house would be time consuming, expensive, and unnecessary.

There were two official change orders issued on the project. Both involved the replacement of sills. The first change order was issued prior to the moving of the house and required the removal and replacement of deteriorated sill beams to ensure structural integrity during transportation and once positioned on the new foundation. The second change order consisted of adding sill beams where none previously existed and the replacement of the existing sills along the south end of the structure, which were found to be in a more deteriorated condition than previously noted prior to the moving operation.

Additional costs were incurred by the structural mover during all the extensions to the schedule. It was the responsibility of the mover to close up and maintain the Joshua Wentworth House to the satisfaction of Strawbery Banke, to pay for all costs incurred to reset and maintain the security alarms, and to adequately protect the new foundation against possible damage due to inclement weather or injury from trespassers and pedestrians.

THE NEW FOUNDATION

The cost of the new foundation was $18,000. Strawbery Banke was open to suggestions on how to reduce expenses in the moving phase so that additional funding could be used in the restoration phase. Any savings by moving the Wentworth House by barge were not passed onto Strawbery Banke, which then sought suggestions on alternative foundation types that may reduce costs. A partial basement or crawl space was suggested, but that solution would be temporary and would need to be replaced in about ten years. It was shown that the future costs would include the disconnection of utilities, temporary raising of the house, demolition of the partial foundation, excavation, construction of a full basement foundation, stonemasonry, reconnection of utilities, and other costs totaling $30,000.

It was also pointed out by the geotechnical engineer that the site consisted of poorly compacted fill down to the level of the cellar floor of the house that once occupied that parcel of land. Verified through research using soil borings and trench tests, the geotechnical engineer warned of a possibility of total or differential settlement of the outer walls of the crawl space foundation due to compaction of the old backfill after the placement of the Wentworth House. He went on to say that the chimneys may also settle because of the relatively small size of the footings in the crawl space situated on the old backfill.

Additional reasons for choosing a full basement foundation were as follows:

1. *Ease of restoration.* Future work on the first-floor framing would be difficult with only a three-foot crawl space to work within. It would require the removal of the flooring to access the framing members below. This would add considerable cost and possible damage to original flooring elements.
2. *Climate control and security.* Heating the building with a forced hot air system, power humidification, and an air-conditioning option would require large ductwork. This would reduce the crawl space headroom to two feet, making inspection of the system and ductwork difficult. The crawl space would also restrict the types of security and monitoring systems that could be installed.
3. *Frame inspection.* Because of the presence of powder post beetles, periodic inspection of the first-floor framing will be necessary. This will be difficult, time consuming, and expensive if restricted to a crawl space.
4. *Structure and chimney inspection.* Since the house is made up of two structures, the constricting size of a crawl space would make it very difficult to inspect and rehabilitate portions of the structure and chimneys.

Ultimately, a full basement foundation utilizing a reinforced-concrete slab on grade with walls was chosen. The only reported change in the foundation layout was the addition of a nine- by two-foot shelf tied into the foundation slab due to the presence of ledge at the southeast corner of the slab.

THE MOVE

After the attached brick Winebaum News building was demolished, the structural mover was able to excavate below the Wentworth House and insert a series of needle beams. Next, two larger main steel beams were threaded below the needle beams, creating a large supporting grid. The house was estimated to weigh 190 tons, fifty of which was the chimney. Because of the weight, the structural mover used a modified ex–tank-retrieving truck to pull the large load. The truck's prior use was to pull trailers carrying armored personnel vehicles and tanks. The mover had modified the truck with steel beams welded perpendicularly to the length of it.

After the house was jacked up enough to allow for the dollies to be attached, the truck was backed into position, and chains were wrapped around the modified truck beams and main beams. Finally, dollies were inserted and attached below the main beams. The house was now ready to go.

On Friday, June 1, 1973, the Joshua Wentworth House began its journey to Strawbery Banke. The house was pulled off its foundation and traveled west along Hanover Street and then turned onto Maplewood Avenue (old Vaughn Street), where it traveled north to Deer Street and down to the pier properties. The house remained at this location over the weekend. Monday morning, an earthen approach was constructed using compacted fill topped off with a combination corrugated metal and timber roadway to allow the truck access onto the barge.

Onlookers standing on the earthen approach and workers watched as the Wentworth House slowly made its way onto the barge that would transport the house down the Piscataqua River and onto the Strawbery Banke property.

With the arrival of the morning high tide, the house was ready to make its way onto the barge. This was the first of two crucial points where Strawbery Banke would accept full responsibility for the welfare of the house during the move, absolving the mover of any responsibility for damages. The house was loaded onto the barge without incident. Because of the unpredictability of water currents, the large main beams were welded onto the deck of the barge as a safety precaution.

With a tug on either side of the barge and another doing the towing, the barge floated down the Piscataqua River and under the Memorial Bridge and docked at Prescott Park, adjacent to Marcy Street.

As critical as when the Wentworth House was pulled onto the barge, pulling it off was just as crucial. Many watched as the Wentworth House was pulled back onto dry land.

The evening high tide allowed the house to be off-loaded, again without incident, and moved closer to Marcy Street, where it waited until the next morning for the final leg of its journey to the end of Hancock Street.

FIGURE 9.8
The Wentworth House being pulled onto the barge.
Courtesy of the Collection of Strawbery Banke Museum, Portsmouth, New Hampshire.

On Tuesday morning, after utility crews cleared the way, the Wentworth House was pulled across Marcy Street, across the parking lot at Strawbery Banke, and down Hancock Street; squeezed around Stoodley's Tavern; and prepared to be situated onto its new foundation.

The structural mover decided to use cribbing as a means of transporting the house over the new foundation and then use reverse jacking to lower the Wentworth House into place.

THE JOSHUA WENTWORTH HOUSE: LESSONS LEARNED

The undertaking of such a huge project with differences in priorities, opinions, and personalities brings to light several lessons that can be learned for this successful project:

1. *Selecting a structural mover.* The selection of the structural mover is the key to the success or failure of your project. Experience is paramount.

If you can hire an experienced structural mover who is not solely interested in the economic aspects of the job but one who enjoys a challenge, you are well on your way to guaranteed success.

2. *Signing a contract.* The contract should cover all aspects of the move. Leave nothing to "let's wait and see what we find." If the house is more than 200 years old, include things such as replacing sills, deteriorated beams, extra interior and exterior support of the structure, condition of masonry chimneys and walls, and insurance in the contract language. What does the insurance cover, and what does it exclude? There must be a clear distinction between the structural mover's responsibilities and what other contractors, such as the foundation contractor, or others involved in the project are responsible for. Consider adding a clause regarding the withholding of final payment until an inspection of the house, once it is situated on the new foundation, has taken place.

3. *Providing insurance.* Confirm what the structural mover's insurance covers and in what amounts. Is the insurance all-inclusive, or is it recommended that you get additional insurance, such as insurance riders? One does not want to become trapped in a moving situation without insurance at a critical part of the project, such as transporting from land to a barge. If the structural mover does not have the confidence and expertise to take full responsibility of this aspect of your project, then you are using the wrong mover.

4. *Acquiring funding.* Be diligent in acquiring all the funding that you are eligible for. Prepare a plan on what the requirements for the success of the project are and follow through with funding. In 2002, funding for preservation was at an all-time high, at least considerably more than in the 1970s. Today the federal government has a number of programs that can be tapped for funding. There is no excuse for not learning about programs and requirements (see chapter 4).

5. *Permitting the new site.* It is imperative to secure all required permits and variances for the new site well in advance of the move. Considerations should be similar to building a new house. Delaying a move may affect the scheduling of other moves by the structural mover, causing your move to be scheduled at a less desirable time.

6. *Considering a preservation consultant.* Many great companies now exist that will represent the home owner or client who is interested in moving a historic structure. With proper contacts and past experience, a

preservation consultant can work with a home owner in assessing historic significance, becoming listed on the National Register, and helping with relocation, restoration, renovation, or rehabilitation efforts.

THE JOSHUA WENTWORTH HOUSE THIRTY YEARS LATER

Resting next to Stoodley's Tavern and across the street from the Daniel Webster House and the Goodwin Mansion, the Wentworth House today looks as if it has existed there all along. The only clue to its journey lies in a small blue and white tablet stating that the house was moved to that location.

There had been considerable planning regarding what the Wentworth House would become once located to the Hancock Street site, but little has been done to make these plans a reality. Over the past thirty years, there have been many presidents, executive vice presidents, directors, and executive directors of Strawbery Banke, all with differing visions and goals for the district, including the Wentworth House.

Plans for the house included the complete restoration of the inside to

FIGURE 9.9
The Joshua Wentworth House as it appeared in August 2003.
Courtesy of the author.

include a gallery on the first floor and part of the second, residential space on the other part of the second and third floors, and a reconstruction of the kitchen on the west side of the house. With additional funding from the public, the National Trust, and the New Hampshire Charitable Fund, the exterior was restored, except the south side (back) of the house, which was done in 1993.

In a 1985 proposal, it was determined that the majority of the costs associated with the restoration of the interior would focus on fire suppression, security, and interior climate control systems. The interior would be stabilized and preserved for future architectural interpretation, providing an appropriate setting for exhibits.

Today, the interior of the Joshua Wentworth House has still not been restored and remains closed to the public. With no current plans for its interior, it is used for storage and the occasional viewing by visiting scholars. The exterior is exhibiting peeling paint and falling or missing clapboards. The chimneys have not been rebuilt since the house was moved and are not visible above the roofline.

With so many buildings on the Strawbery Banke parcel, limited funding has made it difficult to follow through with restoration plans on a number of buildings, including the Joshua Wentworth House. However, Strawbery Banke, a nonprofit historical preservation organization, continues to fight the battle for preservation daily. All one has to do is go to Strawbery Banke and see the many accomplishments of this fine institution. Without organizations such as Strawbery Banke and support from the federal government, preservationists, and concerned citizens, this country's architectural, cultural, economic, political, and social heritage would be buried in the landfills of yesterday.

Moving by Example

This chapter highlights a variety of moves performed by structural movers across the United States. These talented, knowledgeable, and hardworking individuals preserve this country's heritage on a daily basis. Building movers have a sense of pride, dedication, and professionalism unmatched by many professions.

No two moving projects are ever the same. The examples in this chapter were chosen for their content in hopes of bringing the entire moving process together and to demonstrate the inherent challenges and successes of a project, inspiring to relocate and preserve that which is of utmost importance: history.

The movers showcased within this chapter were selected on the basis of their affiliation with the International Association of Structural Movers, their level of experience, and their keen interest in promoting their profession, passed on to them by their ancestors.

FOREST CITY HOUSE

Ron Holland House Moving, Inc.
35545 Highway 69
Forest City, IA 50436
Phone: 641-585-3630; toll free: 877-585-3630
Fax: 641-585-2525
E-mail: info@hollandhousemoving.com
Website: www.hollandhousemoving.com

This neoclassical masonry house possessed a gable roof, a roofline balustrade, and simple square columns. The house, adjacent to Mercy Hospital in Mason City, Iowa, was to be razed to make way for a hospital expansion. It was auctioned off for $750 and moved over thirty miles to Forest City, Iowa.

After holes were made in the masonry foundation, steel beams were threaded under the house to support it during its thirty-mile journey. Next the house was jacked up and rolled off its exiting foundation using three roll beams instead of two as would typically be required for a house of this size. The difference was that the house was made of brick; its weight was much greater than a timber house of the same scale and therefore required an additional set of roll beams.

The house traveled over a portion of Highway 18, carried out after midnight, and then proceeded to Forest City via local roads. Along the way, utility wires were raised and repositioned, and steep hills were negotiated with dollies equipped with brakes, allowing for a controlled descent. Hills can cause many problems in a house move. Ascending and descending a

FIGURE 10.1
Forest City House travels over Interstate 35.
Courtesy of Ron Holland House Moving, Inc.

hill may require additional equipment or equipment specifically designed for hills.

The greater the distance to be traveled, the more important route planning will be. The likelihood of obstructions increases with distance moves, affecting the schedule and causing delays that translate to an increase in costs. In this case, the route from Mason City to Forest City was relatively undeveloped and practically free of any obstructions.

Crossing Interstate 35 required prior authorization from the state department of transportation. To account for permissible axle loads stipulated by the department, the mover had increased the number of dollies to help distribute the load to a number of axles, thus meeting the posted weight limit of the bridge.

Weight plays a major role in any house move. The greater the overall weight of the house, the stronger the steel support system must be to carry that load. This increase in sizes or number of support members will increase the setup and takedown time of the move, which translates to added expenses.

At the new site, the lot is graded and prepared for the arrival of the house. As the house made its way uphill to its final destination, additional tractors pushed and pulled the dollies supporting the steel framework that supported the house into position over the future site of the new foundation. The house was then jacked up to its final position, the dollies and steel support system were removed, and the foundation was constructed up to meet the underside of the house.

SMITH FLAT ROCK HOTEL

Deitz House Moving Engineers, Inc.
2731 Coldstream Court
Muskegon, MI 49444
Phone: 231-773-8964
E-mail: Deitzmovers@aol.com
Website: www.members.aol.com/deitzmovers/index.html

First settled in 1821 by the Vreelandt family of New York State, the area was recorded as Vreelandt, Michigan, in 1834. It was later renamed Smooth Rock after the smooth rock bed of the Huron River, which runs through it. It was not until 1872, when a post office was established, that is was officially named Flat Rock after the Gilbralter & Flat Rock Company, which mapped out an additional area for the town. Finally, in 1923, Flat Rock was incorporated as a village.

The Smith Flat Rock Hotel first opened in October 1896 and was considered a first-class hotel offering meals in the dinning room for thirty-five cents, and residents hoped it would be the cornerstone of the future business district. Built by Lawrence Ferstle, the hotel sat facing Telegraph Road, which ran north to Detroit and south to Toledo, Ohio.

The original Italianate structure possessed decorative overhanging eaves; tall, narrow windows; and two-story porches. In 1999, with the hotel almost certain to be destroyed, the Flat Rock Historical Association decided to have the building relocated.

The first phase of the moving process was to stabilize the structure. The foundation was heavily deteriorated, specifically on the roadway side of the structure, where only a twelve-inch crawl space of limestone and weakened mortar existed. In addition to weathering, the structure's proximity to the roadway (seventeen feet) would have subjected it to road salts and other corrosive elements, deteriorating the brick even further.

All windows and door openings were braced, and cables were wrapped around the entire structure to keep it from coming apart during the moving process.

After excavating to the bottom of the footings, holes were punctured through the foundation using a handheld demolition hammer. Taking into account the fragility of the walls as each square hole was opened, timber blocking was inserted to stabilize adjacent brick from falling away. To effectively install cribbing in the crawl space side, the most sensitive of the entire structure, hand digging was required.

The main beams were inserted through the openings in the foundation. The needle beams were then inserted perpendicular to and on top of the mains. After all the lifting beams and jacks were positioned, the building was raised six feet. With the mains in place, the first set of needle beams were threaded through, with the dollies being installed below the main beams. A total of ten dollies, each with eight wheels, were required to support and transport the structure. The dollies rested on a makeshift road of timber cribbing and plywood. To achieve a level roadway, a combination of shimming, cribbing, plywood, and hand digging and filling was required. Cribbing on the basement portion of the structure was five feet tall while only two feet tall in the crawl space area.

FIGURE 10.2
Smith Flat Rock Hotel.
Courtesy of Daniel Deitz House Moving Engineers, Inc.

Next, the structure with dollies attached was pulled off the original foundation. Stacked cribbing was used as a road for means of egress. The cribbing stacks varied in height to accommodate the differences in grade. To properly orient the building on its new site, the structure required a 130-degree rotation.

With one dolly locked in place, the rest were arced around that point using winch trucks to pull and a loader for anchorage. Once the turn was complete, all the dollies were aligned in the direction of travel, and the structure was ready to begin its journey to the new site.

Arriving at the new site, front loaders pulled the structure, while the front and rear zones of dollies were steered. This final quarter mile consisted of traversing across a soft sod field. With five-foot-wide by fourteen-foot-long oak mud mats as a firm foundation to travel on, the structure arrived safely.

BENSON HALL
Nickel Bros. House Moving, Ltd.
Victoria Office

2060 Mills Road
Sidney, BC V8L 5X4, Canada
Phone: 250-656-2237
Fax: 250-656-8850
E-mail: vic@nickelbros.com
Website: www.nickelbros.com

Built in 1930, the building that would one day be named in honor of
Fr. Glion Benson and become shelter and comfort for those in need was
to be demolished to make way for a new structure. Located on historic
Main Street on Orcas Island, British Columbia, the largest of the San Juan
Islands, the structure had been the home to a number of owners before
the church across the street purchased it in 1979.

After several agreements that would have kept the building in its original location fell through, a prominent citizen from the neighboring Lopez
Island struck a deal with the church to have the building moved to Lopez
Island. The building would be rehabilitated to accommodate office and
retail space and restored to its original exterior appearance.

The project was met with a number of challenges before the move
would even take place. Although many praised the decision to save the
building by moving it off island, there also existed strong opposition
against its removal.

Another challenge that delayed the project was the discovery of midden. Midden is refuse or garbage left from people of the past. Archaeolo-
gists can learn a great deal about past civilizations by what was thrown
away. An archaeologist was present at the site on a daily basis.

Excavation to insert lifting beams moved at a slow pace but was finally
achieved, and the structure was ready to be moved. Moving day began at
6:00 A.M. to take advantage of the high tide. Working quickly, the structural mover pulled the structure away from its original foundation and
drove to the island's eastern shore. With a couple of hundred onlookers
at the barge loading area and a film crew recording the event, the structure
was pulled into position and prepared to be backed onto the waiting
barge.

Because of the steepness of the grade onto the barge, a crane was
hooked to the front of the truck and used to slow the structure's descent
onto the barge. A combination of plywood and cribbing was used to
strengthen the grade leading to the barge. Next, while some workers

waited for the building to be lowered onto the barge, others checked the alignment of the truck wheels to ensure a safe transition onto the steep barge ramp.

After the truck and cargo were aboard, the barge was ready to disembark to Lopez Island, where the journey would be complete in another twenty-four hours, again to take advantage of the high tides.

FIGURE 10.3
The tug boat pulling the barge holding Benson Hall.
Courtesy of Nickel Bros. House Moving, Ltd., British Columbia.

ZOOK HOUSE
Edwards Moving & Rigging, Inc.
2695 Aiken Road
Shelbyville, KY 40065
Phone: 800-404-6064
Fax: 502-722-8093
E-mail: info@edwardsmoving.com
Website: www.edwardsmoving.com

The Jacob Zook House located in Exton, Pennsylvania, was relocated some 200 feet, bringing it closer to Route 30 to clear the way for the adjacent mall's expansion project. The house is included on the National Register of Historic Places and has become a fixture in Exton's history since the early 1700s.

Moritz Zug, or Zook as it was later changed to, a descendant of a very old family in Switzerland, had immigrated as a young man to Berks County and later relocated to Chester Valley. While at Chester Valley, in 1770, Moritz bought 150 acres of land twenty-five miles west of Philadelphia. The land included a spacious sixteen-room farm mansion more than 100 feet in length, originally constructed in 1734.

In addition to its historic significance, the house is a fine example of the Federal architecture that existed in the surrounding townships at the time. The house is comprised of two-foot-thick stone walls, a hip roof with gable ends, and a first floor supported by hand-hewn eight-square-inch walnut beams. The house has undergone a number of additions and interior modifications but had remained on its original footprint for more than 260 years.

The project consisted of moving the 650-ton house 200 feet across the mall access road and onto its new foundation. This may have seemed simple at first, but, as with all aged masonry structures, particularly of variously sized stone and mortar facades, the task proved to be quite delicate and unpredictable.

The first task was to dig around the house to expose the foundation. It became obvious as the cutting for the penetrations proceeded that the two-foot-thick walls of the house were badly deteriorated and crumbling. It was decided that timber blocks or cribbing of varying sizes would be wedged between the needle beams and the underside of the house walls for support.

First, large 100-foot steel I-beam mains were threaded below the length of the house and set on cribbing. Next, twenty-four steel beams were inserted at four-foot intervals along the length of the house, perpendicular to the main beams. Some needle beams penetrated the web, while others simply rested on the top flanges of the main beams.

The weight of the house was supported on twenty-two jacks, intermittently spaced along the length of the main beams. After the structure was secured and shimmed properly, it was raised to height of eight feet. Next, dollies were inserted below the raised structure and attached to various members of the steel support grid, and then the structure was lowered onto the dollies and prepared for moving.

Because of the structure's age and fragile condition, the house was moved at a snail's pace to the new site. To negotiate the various slopes and soil conditions, oak mud mats and gravel were used to provide a firm base for the dollies to travel on.

Once over the new foundation slab, masonry walls were constructed up to meet the underside of the walls of the house to prevent any cracking of walls, which is common if a structure of this age and state is lowered onto a perfectly level foundation.

An archeological dig was performed prior to and after the Zook house was moved. Along with two buried wells and the remains of an old foundation, additional items found included beads, straight pins, buttons, ceramics, and coins. All the findings can help piece together what life was like in the mid-1700s.

Today, the Jacob Zook House stands proudly among modern-day

FIGURE 10.4
The Zook House.
Courtesy of Edwards Moving & Rigging, Inc., Shelbyville, Kentucky.

buildings and structures, reminding us of a time when roads were less traveled and life was set at a much slower pace.

THE 1928 ADDISON MIZNER MANSION
Modern House & Building Movers, Inc.
14405 Congress Street
Orlando, FL 32826
Phone: 407-677-1440
Fax: 407-977-8681
E-mail: info@modermovers.com
Website: www.modernmovers.com

Addison Mizner was Florida's leading architect in the 1920s. Spending most of his childhood in Spain and Central America, Mizner was able to establish his own Spanish and Mediterranean Revival-style architecture. At the height of his career, Mizner designed over fifty Palm Beach villas and Florida mansions for the nation's elite social families.

The 1928 Addison Mizner Mansion, know as "L'Encantada" (the Enchanted One), was designed for the first mayor of Manalapan. The house was one of the last homes that Mizner designed and the only one in Manalapan. One of the most expensive moves in the United States, the 8,000-square-foot mansion contained twenty-five rooms, ceiling murals, frescoes, stone carvings, and cypress doors. The structure was comprised of hollow clay tile, masonry, mortar, and stucco and weighed over 1,000 tons intact.

The mansion was purchased as real estate investment by one of the wealthiest men in the country. It was to be torn down, and two 16,000-square-foot homes were to be constructed in its place. After learning that the mansion was to be destroyed, a young girl, having previously visited the house, once home to a friend, pleaded with her father to save the mansion from destruction. Her father, an affluent real estate developer himself, and his partner purchased the home for $3.2 million with the intent of moving it to rescue it from the wrecking ball.

The plan was to cut the horseshoe-shaped Palm Beach mansion in three pieces, put them on a barge, and float them eighty miles up the Intracoastal Waterway to a three-acre lot at Bay Tree Island in Seawall's Point.

With a moving deadline fast approaching and a week of weather-related delays, the first and largest section of the house, two stories high and weighing 300 tons, was loaded onto a 140-foot barge using two front-end loaders. The barge was then towed by two tugboats and escorted by a specialized boat that could be anchored to the sea bottom. Almost immediately, the wind shifted direction, and the tugboat ran aground less than 100 yards from its original site. At the next high tide, the barge was on its way to Seawall's Point.

The Seawall's Point Zoning Board of Adjustment required a setback variance to issue a building permit. The owners resolved that dilemma by updating the plans, which reflected the removal of a portion of the mansion built in 1985, and relocating it slightly south of its original location, thus meeting the setback requirement. Next, Seawall's Point residents challenged the validity of the claim that the house was designed by Addison Mizner. The owners were forced into obtaining a letter of authenticity verifying that the mansion was in fact Addison Mizner's work.

With additional resistance by local residents and possible fines by the Department of Environmental Protection (DEP) of $10,000 a day for any

FIGURE 10.5
The last two portions of the Mizner Mansion are offloaded at the Palm Beach site.
Courtesy of Modern House & Building Movers, Inc., Chuluota, Florida.

damage to the endangered Johnson sea grass while attempting to offload the house onto the Seawall's Point site, the owners decided to look for another site.

The deadline for removing the house off the original site was extended, and the owners continued to battle for almost a year with officials of Seawall's Point for permission to place the home on the planned Intracoastal Waterway site near Manalapan. The DEP denied permission to the site, citing potential damage to sea grass, mangroves, tropical trees, and shrubbery.

In a last-ditch effort, the owners were then able to convince the Harbor Branch Oceanographic Institute, near Fort Pierce, to allow the structure to be housed there for ninety days. In return, the owners made a $50,000 donation to the institute.

Next, the second section of the Mizner Mansion, weighing 220 tons, was barged to Harbor Branch without incident. The last section proved to be the most costly of the three. Weighing 300 tons and supported on twelve dollies, crews worked through the night using giant light towers to make up for the three-day delay while waiting for a larger barge to be shipped down from Jacksonville. The DEP insisted on using a larger barge with a shallower draft (the amount of the barge below water level) to distribute the weight over a larger surface area, preventing the barge from sinking deeper into the water and disturbing the sea grass.

During the early morning high tide, the barge was loaded, but it was too heavy and became lodged in the sea bottom. With four large front-end loaders pushing and two tugboats pulling, the barge still would not move. It was decided that one-inch steel cables at a cost of $10,000 would be connected to four sixty-ton tow trucks on Hypoluxo Island across the channel, with two front-end loaders pushing from the other end. Their efforts were successful, and the last piece of the mansion was towed to Harbor Branch Oceanographic Institute.

Over the next several months while looking for a new site, the DEP fined the owners $86,000 for destroying nearly one and a half acres of Johnson sea grass while the mansion was being barged off the original site near Manalapan. The owner of the old site where the mansion once stood also charged the new owners $85,000 for storage fees.

After surviving hurricane season in three pieces at Harbor Branch, a site was finally found in Palm Beach, less than a mile from the original site. After turtle nesting season was over and a large number of zoning variances had been approved, the first section of the Mizner Mansion was ready to be barged to its new $6.5 million location.

Once again, weather played a factor in the move. The owners were forced to moor the first section of the house at the Port of Palm Beach at the cost of $1,000 a day until the weather cleared.

As the first barge arrived carrying the 420-ton section of the Mizner Mansion, finishing touches were made to the ramp that would connect the barge to shore. The temporary ramp was constructed using timber and native sand and steel I beams to support the large steel plates that would be used as a makeshift road on which the house would travel. The sixty-foot-wide section was pulled across the steel plates by four cables connected to winches on two trucks, both anchored by front-end loaders. After waiting to cross the main road, the first section was pulled into position over sixty-one concrete piles buried to a depth of thirty feet, similar to the ones constructed at the original move site. Concrete piles are columns that are buried to act as a solid foundation to support the structure. If soil is washed away, the piles will continue to support the house, avoiding a collapse.

Next, the last two portions of the house, weighing over 600 tons, were floated together to the new site after being moored for more than a week at the Port of Palm Beach because of weather delays. After a ten-month journey up and down the Intracoastal Waterway and after some repositioning of the barge, the sections were pulled ashore and placed into position.

After tugboats, specialized craft, a team of structural movers, consultants, a documentary crew, throngs of media, curious onlookers, and a price tag of well over $12 million in the end, the house met its demise by the manner in which owners tried to avoid in the first place: the wrecking ball. After a long and bitter lawsuit between the owners of the property, key architectural treasures within the mansion were purchased and removed, and the house was destroyed.

KING OF PRUSSIA INN

International Chimney Corporation
55 South Long Street
Williamsville, NY 14221

Phone: 716-634-3967
Fax: 716-634-3983
E-mail: info@internationalchimney.com
Website: www.internationalchimney.com

Located in southeastern Pennsylvania, the King of Prussia Inn, one of Pennsylvania's most historically significant buildings, had remained isolated for fifty years on the median strip of U.S. Route 202, just north of the I-76 interchange.

The inn was built around 1719 and remodeled in 1750 and again in 1769. It was named for Frederick the Great of Prussia, who had helped the British defeat the French during the French and Indian War. The inn was in the path of various Revolutionary armies and played host to many important military figures. The inn was located within a day's travel by horse from nearby Philadelphia, and records at the inn indicated that General George Washington stayed and held meetings there.

This simple Georgian-style two-and-a-half-story inn has a side gable roof and a two-story porch (added later) running across the north facade. The building is comprised of stuccoed fieldstone, and its present appearance is largely the same as it was after its 1769 enlargement.

Through the efforts of the King of Prussia Historical Society, the inn was listed on the National Register in 1975. A covenant between the King of Prussia Historical Society, the inn's owner, and the Pennsylvania Bureau for Historic Preservation was formed to safeguard the structure and explore stabilization and restoration programs.

In the mid-1990s, the Pennsylvania Department of Transportation (PennDOT) acquired almost thirty acres of private land, increasing its right-of-way for widening Route 202. Following a feasibility study, an agreement to relocate the inn was struck between the PennDOT, the Federal Highway Administration, the Pennsylvania Bureau for Historic Preservation, and the Advisory Council on Historic Preservation. The move was tentatively scheduled for the summer of 1998, but the highway project was delayed indefinitely because of a lack of funding.

Four years later, with the highway-widening project on a fast track, the King of Prussia Chamber of Commerce, now owners of the inn, were initially looking into dismantling the building and moving it. After consulting with several agencies, it was decided that the building would be moved intact.

Before preparations for moving the structure could begin, a team from PennDOT conducted an archaeological investigation of the inn site, gathering as much information about the inn's buried past as possible.

The inn weighed approximately 580 tons and was extremely fragile. There are several factors that contributed to the severe deterioration of the structure. When the inn was constructed, cement had not yet been invented. The mixture that held the fieldstone walls together consisted of lime and sand. This weak binding material, in combination with the age of the structure and the sanding and salting of Route 202 on either side of the Inn, had resulted in the structure's poor condition.

First, the entire structure was reinforced using extensive timber shoring and bracing. All openings, including windows and doors, were reinforced with timber frames, and the entire structure was wrapped with steel cables to maintain its structural integrity.

Next, the inn's foundation walls were exposed by slowly excavating, shoring, and bracing the walls, keeping them structurally intact. Once stability of the foundation walls had been achieved, the foundation was saw-cut in a number of locations, and the main steel, cross steel, and needle beams were installed under the structure.

Using a Unified™ Jacking Machine, the structure was lifted in six-inch increments over a number of weeks to minimize adverse effects to the structure. Once the building was at the proper height for travel, additional cribbing was added in the basement on which twenty-one dollies were placed and secured to the bottom of the mains. The cribbing acted as ramps on which the inn would travel off its existing foundation and onto Route 202. Once under way, the structure and supporting framing were constantly monitored.

Adding to the challenges of the project, the King of Prussia area is prone to sinkholes. A sinkhole is a depression caused by the soil and other materials subsiding into an open hole or void below the ground surface, similar to the way sand from an hourglass passes from the top to the bottom. Like the hourglass, a depression or subsidence occurs at the surface when enough sand or soil moves into the deeper void.

Holes measuring up to 150 feet deep were encountered on other nearby sections of the Route 202 project. The inn's travel route also had a couple of sinkholes open up while the structure was being prepared for its journey. In anticipation of sinkholes, PennDOT had set up a grout production

FIGURE 10.6
The King of Prussia Inn makes its way over the bridge at Abram's Run in the
presence of local media and hundreds of onlookers.

facility on the project site. Grout is a mortar mix that is used to fill in narrow openings in a variety of applications. The grout on this project was used to fill in the sinkholes.

The length of the move was approximately one mile. A strict moving time frame, with penalties of up to $10,000 for every hour over the time limit, was in effect to ensure minimal disruptions to vehicular traffic. Negotiating a number of sharp turns required constant adjusting of the dollies, one turn taking several hours to complete.

This bridge on the travel path had a posted weight limit far below the required capacity to support the building and its network of steel support beams. It had to be reinforced using steel pipe columns welded to the underside of the steel beams and supported on the existing substructure of the bridge to minimize settlement.

In addition, to help distribute the applied loads, cribbing was placed along the bridge deck on which the dollies would travel. This additional six inches of height also made it possible for the steel members supporting the inn to clear the concrete bridge railing.

Once the inn was positioned over the location of its new foundation, cribbing was added to support the inn while the dollies and mains were removed. Next, the foundation was constructed up to meet the underside of the structure. The needle beams were finally removed, the holes were closed up, and the foundation was backfilled.

Bibliography

INTRODUCTION, CHAPTERS 1 AND 2

Beaver Island Historical Society. "History of Beaver Island." 23 December 2003. www.beaverisland.net/history/.

Curtis, John O. *Moving Historic Buildings*. Washington, D.C.: U.S. Department of the Interior Heritage Conservation and Recreation Service, Technical Preservation Services Division, 1979.

Doyle, Tom. President of the International Association of Structural Movers. Telephone interview. 16 December 2003.

Follett, Jean A. The Hotel Pelham: A New Building Type for America. *American Art Journal* 15, no. 4 (autumn 1983): 58–73.

How to Move Houses. *American Agriculturalist*, 32 November 1873, 417–18.

Paravalos, Peter, and Wayne H. Kalayjian. Moving an Historic Lighthouse. *Journal of the Boston Society of Civil Engineers Section/ASCE* 12, no. 2 (1997): 5–17.

Schweitzer, Sarah. "Barns, and a Sense of Place, May Vanish." *Boston Globe*, 20 January 2003, Metro/Region, A1.

Stevenson, David. *House Moving: Sketch of the Civil Engineering of North America*. London: John Weale, Burns Library, Boston College, 1838.

Tuxill, Carl A. Past Publisher for *The Structural Mover* Magazine. Telephone interview. 12 December 2003.

Vertical House Moving. *Scientific American*, 12 December 1903, 446 + .

CHAPTERS 3 AND 4

Beers, Peter. Pope-Leighey House. 23 December 2003. www.peterbeers.net/interests/flw_rt/Virginia/pope_leighey/pope_leighey.h tm.

Boyle, Jayne F., Stuart Ginsberg, and Sally G. Oldham. *A Guide to Tax-Advantaged Rehabilitation*. Washington, D.C.: National Trust for Historic Preservation, 2002.

City of Santa Monica, Calafornia. Public Works Department. Telephone interview. 25 March 2003. http://pen.ci.santa-monica.ca.us/municode/codemaster/
article_7/36/.

City of West Palm Beach, Florida. Construction Services Department. Telephone
interview. 25 March 2003. www.cityofwpb.com/construction/.

City of Windsor Heights, Iowa. Public Works Department. Telephone interview.
25 March 2003. www.winsorheights.org/citycode.html.

Cornish, Joseph. Stewardship Manager of the Society for the Preservation of New
England Antiquities. Personal interview. 12 December 2003.

Cornish, Joseph, and Susanna Crampton. Just around the Corner. *Historic New
England, The Magazine of the Society for the Preservation of New England Antiquities*, winter 2003/spring 2004, 20.

Heritage Preservation Services. National Park Service. April 2002. www2.cr.nps
.gov/welcome.htm.

Marks, Philip, III. Atlantic Aeolus. Personal interview. 19 June 2002.

National Park Service. *Illustrated Guidelines for Rehabilitating Historic Buildings.*
Washington, D.C.: Historic Preservation Services, 1992.

———. *The Secretary of the Interior's Standards for Rehabilitation.* Washington,
D.C.: Historic Preservation Services, 1990.

National Trust for Historic Preservation. September 2002. www.nationaltrust.org.

Quinn Evans Architects. Pope-Leighey House. 23 December 2003. www.quin
nevans.com/projects/pope.html.

Town of Norton, Massachusetts, Building Department. Telephone interview. 25
March 2003.

Tuminaro, Craig. Associate Director of Preservation Programs, Frank Lloyd
Wright's Pope-Leighey House of the National Trust for Historic Preservation.
Personal interview. 3 November 2003.

Tyler, Norman. *Historic Preservation.* New York: Norton, 2000.

Weeks, Kay D., and Anne E. Grimmer. *The Secretary of the Interior's Standards for
the Treatment of Historic Properties.* Washington, D.C.: U.S. Department of the
Interior, National Park Service, 1995.

CHAPTERS 5 AND 6

Barber, Stan. Larmon House Movers. Personal interview. 12 June 2002.

Becker, Norman. *The Complete Book of Home Inspection.* 2nd ed. Washington,
D.C.: McGraw, 1993.

Betts, Don. D. R. Betts Building Movers. Personal interview. 17 June 2003.

Brown, Anthony D. Mobile Crane Inspection Guidelines for OSHA Compliance
Officers. U.S. Department of Labor Occupational Safety and Health Adminis-

tration. June 1994. www.osha-sle.gov/SLTC/cranehoistsafety/mobilecrane/mobil crane_1.html.

Bucher, Ward, ed. *Dictionary of Building Preservation*. New York: Wiley, 1996, 28–29.

Edelstien, David. 110 Year Old Antique Store Is Refurbished. *The Structural Mover Magazine*, April 2001, 28–29.

Edwards, Mark. Move Condos. *The House and Building Mover*, January 1995, 4 + .

Federal Emergency Management Administration. *Above the Flood: Elevating Your Floodprone House*. FEMA Publication 347, May 2000.

Get-a-quote.net. Hydraulic Truck Cranes. 4 January 2004. www.get-a-quote.net.

Hayden, Bob. Hayden Building Movers. Personal interview. 19 June 2003.

Kennedy, Hollis, and Keith Kennedy. Moving the Mars Stone Chapel—Pulaski, Tennessee. *The Structural Mover Magazine*, September 2003, 10–14.

Knaebe, Mike. General Manger for Hevi-Haul International, Ltd. Personal interview. 7 November 2003.

Lindsay, Dennis R. Lindsay Moving & Rigging, Inc. *The House and Building Mover*, April 1996, 4 + .

McAlester, Virginia, and Lee McAlester. *A Field Guide to American Houses*. New York: Knopf, 1984.

McCulloch, Laurie. Utilities versus Moving. *The Structural Mover Magazine*, September 2003, 18–20.

Nash, George. *Renovating Old Houses*. Newtown, Conn.: Taunton Press, 1992.

Smith, Anita Carol. So You Want to Rent a Crane? *San Diego Metropolitan Magazine*, January 2004. www.sandiegometro.com.

Thallon, Rob. *Graphic Guide to Frame Construction*. Newtown, Conn.: Taunton Press, 1996.

CHAPTER 7

Cox Communications. Rhode Island Cable Company. Telephone interview. 10 April 2003.

Hotton, Peter C. The Hard Part of Moving a House Is Getting Ready. *Boston Globe*, 3 February 1985, B99. http://register.bostonglobe.com/archives2/cgi-bin/archives.cgi.

Michaels, Julie. The Cost of Relocating a Free House Can Add Up Pretty Quickly. *Boston Globe*, 5 February 1998, F1. http://register.bostonglobe.com/archives2/cgi-bin/archives.cgi.

Narragansett Electric. Rhode Island Electric Company. Telephone interview. 10 April 2003.

Northeast Utilities. Connecticut Electric Company. Telephone interview. 10 April 2003.

Pollard, Gayle. Moving Lock, Stock, Barrel—and House. *Boston Globe*, 7 May 1982. http://register.bostonglobe.com/archives2/cgi-bin/archives.cgi.

Verizon. New Hampshire Telephone Company. Telephone interview. 10 April 2003.

Verizon. Vermont Telephone Company. Telephone interview. 10 April 2003.

Water and Sewer Departments, Attleboro, Massachusetts. Telephone interview. 10 April 2003.

Water and Sewer Departments, Norton, Massachusetts. Telephone interview. 10 April 2003.

Winslow Marine Inc. Tug and Barge Services, Falmouth Maine. David Winslow, President. Telephone interview. 25 September 2003.

CHAPTER 8

Awaiting Street Move. *Portsmouth Herald*, 5 June 1973, late ed., 1.

Bond, Cynthia. Portsmouth Legacy. *New Hampshire Century.Com*, 20 September 2003. www.nhcentury.com/portsmouth/porleg/strbanmus.com.

Bottomley, William Lawrence, ed. *Great Georgian Houses of America*. Vol. 2. New York: Scribner, 1937.

Carse, Robert. *Ports of Call*. New York: Scribner, 1967.

Conors, Timothy (Ted) J., Past Mayor (1973) of Portsmouth, New Hampshire, Administrator, Portsmouth Housing Authority. Telephone interview. 26 September 2003.

Fenwick, Mrs. Marston. Old House Rejuvenated. *Portsmouth Herald*, 16 August 1958, late ed., 1–2.

Harry Winebaum Remembers. *Portsmouth Herald*, 5 June 1973, late ed., 2.

Heritage on the March. *Portsmouth Herald*, 26 February 1963, late ed., 12.

House Rides the Piscataque. *Portsmouth Herald*, 4 June 1973, late ed., 1.

Howells, John Mead. *The Architectural Heritage of the Piscataqua, Houses and Gardens of the Portsmouth District of Maine and New Hampshire*. New York: Architectural Book Publishing Company, 1937.

Job Nearing End. *Portsmouth Herald*, 6 June 1973, late ed., 1.

Letters of Henry E. Parker. *Rootsweb.Com*. Letter, 3 January 1873, 9 October 2003. http://freepages.genealogy.rootsweb.com/henryparker/hanover_letters_files/nh_history.htm.

Old Tavern Poses "Emergency" for Banke, Historic Building Faces Wrecker's Hammers. *Portsmouth Herald*, 15 August 1954, late ed., 8.

Rogers, Lisa. When Memories Collide: Strawbery Banke Tells the History of Neighbors. National Endowment for the Humanities. 14 October 2003. http://neh.gov/news/humanities/1999-01/shapiro.html.

Schmitt, Beth Ann. Educator for Public Programs of the Society for the Preservation of New England Antiquities. Personal interview. 21 September 2003.
———. Moving History. Society for the Preservation of New England Antiquities. Governor John Langdon House, Portsmouth, New Hampshire. 21 September 2003.
Strawbery Banke, Inc. *Strawbery Banke Official Guidebook*. 2nd ed. Portsmouth, N.H.: Peter E. Randall Publisher, 2002.

CHAPTER 9

Forest City House

Hammer, Natalie. Holland House Moving. E-mail interview. 3 December 2003.
Hollandhousemoving.com. 3 December 2003.

Smith Flat Rock Hotel

Deitz, Daniel. Deitz House Moving Engineers, Inc. Telephone interview. 15 December 2003.
———. Historic Preservation. *The Structural Mover Magazine*, September 2000, 20–23. *Members.aol.com/deitzmovers/index.html*. 15 December 2003.
Davis, Karen Jolly. Landmark Moved from Island/Delicate Operation Puts Coast Guard Station on Barge for Trip to New Site. *Norfolk Virginian-Pilot*, 1 May 1998. www.welcome.hamptonroads.com/archives/.

Benson Hall

Connelly, Jim. Nickel Bros. House Moving. Telephone interview. 13 December 2003.
DeBin, Debi. Nickel Bros. House Moving. Telephone interview. 12 December 2003.
Grossman, Ted. From Orcas, to Lopez, with Love. *The Island's Sounder*, 19 February 2002. www.islandssounder.com/portals-code/searchd.cgi.
Nickelbros.com. 19 December 2003.

Zook House

Crawford, John. History in Motion. *Daily Local News*, 30 September 1998, early ed., A1, A4, C1.
Edwards, Mark. Telephone interview. 14 December 2003.
Edwards, Stephen. E-mail interview. 3 December 2003.
Edwardsmoving.com. 3 December 2003.

Mast (Zook), Lois Ann. E-mail interview. 22 December 2003.

Sharp, John. Mennonite Church USA Historical Committee. E-mail interview. 22 December 2003.

Zook, Lois Ann. *Only a Twig.* Lancaster, Pa.: Lois Ann Zook, 1979.

The 1928 Addison Mizner Mansion

Burdett, Pat. Modern House Movers. Telephone interview. 10 December 2003.

Caputo, Marc. Penalties Diverge in Seafloor Scrapes. *Palm Beach Post,* 25 October 2000. http://nl.newsbank.com/nl-search/we/archives.

Cooper, William, Jr. Mizner Mansion Piece Settles onto Its New Lot. *Palm Beach Post,* 4 February 2001. http://nl.newsbank.com/nl-search/we/archives.

Davies, Dani. First Piece of Mansion Ends 18-Hour Trek. *Palm Beach Post,* 22 April 2000. http://nl.newsbank.com/nl-search/we/archives.

Doig, Mathew. Hurricane Season Poses New Threat to Mizner Mansion. *Palm Beach Post,* 16 August 2000. http://nl.newsbank.com/nl-search/we/archives.

———. Mansion Move Will Begin Again Next Week. *Palm Beach Post,* 5 May 2000. http://nl.newsbank.com/nl-search/we/archives.

———. Man's Mission: Use Intercoastal to Move Mansion. *Palm Beach Post,* 23 January 2000. http://nl.newsbank.com/nl-search/we/archives.

———. Mizner Mansion Closing in on Move to Sewall's Point. *Palm Beach Post,* 3 March 2000. http://nl.newsbank.com/nl-search/we/archives.

———. Mizner Mansion's Owner Given Time to Relocate House. *Palm Beach Post,* 26 January 2000. http://nl.newsbank.com/nl-search/we/archives.

———. Owners of Mizner Mansion Fined $86,000 for Damaging Sea Grass. *Palm Beach Post,* 25 August 2000. http://nl.newsbank.com/nl-search/we/archives.

Eisenhauer, Sarah. Mizner Mansion May Be Leaving. *Palm Beach Post,* 15 September 2000. http://nl.newsbank.com/nl-search/we/archives.

Hartnett, William M. Mansion Gets Extended Stay at Harbor Branch. *Palm Beach Post,* 7 July 2000. http://nl.newsbank.com/nl-search/we/archives.

King, Robert P. Part Two of Mizner Mansion at Final Site. *Palm Beach Post,* 18 February 2001. http://nl.newsbank.com/nl-search/we/archives.

McCabe, Scott. High Mizner House Movers Find Rough Going. *Palm Beach Post,* 20 April 2000. http://nl.newsbank.com/nl-search/we/archives.

Modernmovers.com. 3 December 2003.

O'Meilia, Tim. Biggest Chunk of Mizner Mansion Almost Home. *Palm Beach Post,* 2 February 2001. http://nl.newsbank.com/nl-search/we/archives.

———. Final Two Sections of Mizner Mansion to Head Together Down Intercoastal Today. *Palm Beach Post,* 8 February 2001. http://nl.newsbank.com/nl-search/we/archives.

————. Last Section of Mizner House Afloat. *Palm Beach Post*, 17 May 2000. http://nl.newsbank.com/nl-search/we/archives.

————. Ongoing Mansion Rolls Ashore. *Palm Beach Post*, 3 February 2001. http://nl.newsbank.com/nl-search/we/archives.

————. Roving Mizner Mansion to Be Razed. *Palm Beach Post*, 26 April 2001. http://nl.newsbank.com/nl-search/we/archives.

King of Prussia Inn

Internationalchimney.com. 20 December 2003.

Pribble, Mark. International Chimney. Telephone interview. 24 December 2003.

————. What Made The King of Prussia Inn Relocation Unique? *The Structural Mover Magazine*, April 2001, 20–25.

Index

About the Author

Peter Paravalos is a structural engineer with experience in design, inspection, assessment, restoration, and rehabilitation of various historic, transportation, and public works facilities. He currently sits on a number of historic commissions for his hometown of Norton, Massachusetts.